"To Discourage Me Is No Easy Matter":
The Life of California Pioneer William Goodwin Dana

By
Joseph L. Dana

Written for the South County Historical Society
Arroyo Grande, California
2007

First Edition, Copyright © 2007 by the South County Historical Society, P.O. Box 633, Arroyo Grande, CA 93421

Cover and layout design by Sand Dollar Marketing.

ISBN 0-9673464-7-9

Acknowledgments:

The following are printed with the permission of the Dana Adobe Nipomo Amigos (DANA): Maria Josefa Carrillo, Dana Adobe (2 exterior and 1 interior), Adelina's burial site, William and Josefa Dana's graves, Maria Josefa Tefft Pollard, History of the Dana Brand, William Dana family chart, chart of William and Maria Josefa's children and spouses, Dana Adobe before restoration and volunteers making adobe bricks.

The following are printed with the permission of the South County Historical Society: Juan Francisco Dana, Cave Landing.

The photograph of John Rogers Cooper is reprinted with permission from Boxwood Publications.

Table of Contents

Note from the Author

Exactly twenty-one years ago, I began this book. At the time, I was a senior majoring in history at the University of California at Berkeley. Faced with the requirement of writing a senior thesis, I selected a topic close to my heart: a historical biography of my great-great-grandfather, William Goodwin Dana.

The thesis turned out to be the most exciting research experience of my life. I happily spent hours and hours amid the stacks of the Doe Library and in the reading room of the Bancroft Library searching for every tidbit I could find on Dana. Some of my discoveries were especially meaningful: I still remember the thrill of touching – with my own hands! – letters penned a century and a half earlier by the man himself.

I left Berkeley intending to eventually expand my thesis into a brief book about Dana. Work, family, and other commitments have kept me from doing this for some time, so I am extremely honored and pleased that the South County Historical Society has given me the encouragement to make my longtime dream a reality. This book is intended to provide a synthesis of the writings and other primary source material available on Dana. Hopefully, those who read it will come away with some new insights into his distinguished life. Hopefully, it also will inspire others to do even more research on Dana, his family, and his times.

Finally, I would like to express my deep, heartfelt thanks to everyone who has encouraged me to write this book. I am especially indebted to the following people:

• Jon Gjerde, my thesis adviser at Berkeley;

• James D. Hart, the former Bancroft Library curator who in 1989 gave me some inspirational advice and entered my thesis into the Bancroft Library collection;

• Lisa Vanderstad and Herb Kandel of the Dana Adobe Nipomo Amigos;

• Thomas Wheeler of the Dana Adobe Nipomo Amigos, who generously shared his valuable research on Dana's life in Hawaii;

• The members of the Book Committee of the South County Historical Society;

• Linda Shephard of the South County Historical Society, who has been a perceptive editor;

• Barbara Watson of the Dana Adobe Nipomo Amigos, who is the godmother of this book; and

• All of my fellow Danas, especially George Dana; my parents, David and Susan Dana; my wife, Angelina Dana; and my children, Jacob and Sabrina Dana.

This book is dedicated to all of the descendants of William Goodwin Dana.

Joseph L. Dana
September 2007

Preface

As for any other historical figure, the life of William Goodwin Dana can be viewed from a multitude of perspectives. By any account, Dana can be seen as one of the most prominent and consequential people in the history of early California. From learning about Dana, one also can study him as a pioneer, an adventurer, an entrepreneur, a person who overcomes childhood adversity, a public servant, even the author of some incredibly captivating letters. This brief biography will cover these angles, but the emphasis in recounting Dana's life will be to take a cultural perspective. The details, quotes, anecdotes, letters, and historical interpretations have been chosen not just to describe what Dana saw and did, but to illustrate the contrast of cultures he negotiated throughout his life. During the course of his 60 years Dana went from being a New England Yankee to a seafaring adventurer to a land grantee in Mexican California to a citizen of the United States once again. He underwent many other transformations: from William to Guillermo, from Congregationalist to Catholic, from Captain to Don. William Goodwin Dana lived at the epicenter of continuous change, and this book will tell that story.

William Goodwin Dana

Cambridge to Canton: 'Buffeting Old Neptune'

William Goodwin Dana's lineage traces back to early colonial times. Richard Dana, the progenitor of the Dana family in America, was born in Manchester, England, in 1617. He arrived in New England in 1640 at the age of 23, during a time "when many other young men from the same part of England were … settling in the same part of New England."[1] This destination was Cambridge, Massachusetts, where Dana was among the town's original settlers. Shortly after receiving a land grant in 1647 in what was then called "Little Cambridge" (now part of Brighton, just west of Boston), Richard married Anne Bullard, who herself had come to America with her parents from England in 1635. The two had 12 children, thus establishing numerous branches on the Dana family tree.

The Danas were well known and well established in Cambridge and nearby Boston, and it is no coincidence that several of Richard's descendants played important roles in the seminal event of the period, the American Revolution. Among them were Judge Richard Dana, who, as one of the original members of the Sons of Liberty, was active in blocking the enforcement of the Stamp Act; Captain Stephen Dana, who commanded a company of soldiers in General George Washington's Continental Army; and

Francis Dana, a lawyer, delegate to the Continental Congress, and diplomat who later became one of the framers of the Articles of Confederation.

The revolution played a central role in the lives of William Goodwin's parents and grandparents. Benjamin Dana, a great-grandson of Richard, was born in Cambridge in 1741. He married Lucy Whitney in 1766, and a year

Elizabeth Dana   **William Dana**

later their first child, William, was born. William was a boy during the Revolution, when his father served as a lieutenant in his relative Stephen Dana's company. No information on William's education and career is available; all that is known is that he married Elizabeth Davis, eldest daughter of Boston Tea Party participant and Continental Army officer Major Robert Davis, on December 8, 1796. William was 29; Elizabeth was 18. On May 5, 1797, their first child, a boy named William Goodwin, was born. William was baptized by Rev. Dr. Joseph Lathrop, a Congregationalist from West Springfield, on May 17, 1797.[2]   William and Elizabeth's second child, Adeline Eliza, was born on June 12, 1798.

William Goodwin's formative years took place amid death and tragedy. He was just two when his father died. William Dana apparently had been very ill during his son's childhood; on June 3, 1799, he died in St. Thomas, West Indies, where he reportedly had gone to improve his health.[3]   He was buried in St. Thomas, with a friend setting down "a stone in his memory."[4]   Widowed at 21, William's mother remarried three years later, on September 25, 1802. William's new stepfather was Captain Thomas Chandler, a Harvard graduate, and the family settled in Worcester, Massachusetts.   Elizabeth bore Captain Chandler one child, a girl named Theoda who died in infancy. After less than two years of marriage, Captain Chandler died, leaving Elizabeth a widow again at the age of 26. William's mother married for the third time on December 8, 1805, this time to Captain James Rowan. Less than a year later, Elizabeth herself died in Worcester on October 16, 1806, leaving William and Adeline orphans at the ages of nine and eight respectively. Elizabeth was buried in Worcester.

Nothing is known about who took care of William and Adeline immediately following the death of their mother, although one source reports that he was able to acquire a "good education."[5]   The trying times evidently brought brother and sister closer together. Adeline, in a December 29, 1825, letter to William, referred to the hardship they had experienced: "I feel, my beloved Brother, that there is a peculiar nearness in the tie which binds us to each other, deprived as we both have been at an early period of our love of our natural Protector's [sic] and without other near natural claims upon our hearts. ... We must be more dependant [sic] for happiness upon each other, than if we had a wider circle of family ties among whom our affections should diffuse themselves so let me have a constant place in your memory."[6]

* * *

One of the formative influences on young William was his uncle William Heath Davis, a prominent ship owner engaged in trade with numerous ports in the Pacific. Davis acted as a mentor to William and helped his nephew launch a career at sea. According to historian Andrew F. Rolle, Davis' primary business was the traffic of sandalwood between the Sandwich Islands (present-day Hawaii), China, and other ports. Writes Rolle, "Because the Revolutionary War had deprived American merchants of the imperial trade preferences they once enjoyed, such men were forced to seek new markets in the Pacific. This search for trade outlets led Captain Davis, as it did many of his contemporary New Englanders, both to Hawaii and to the docks of Canton, China."[7]   Continues Rolle, "Captain Davis first entered the China trade in 1807. ... For more than ten years the captain engaged in highly successful commercial operations including the China trade, business with the Russians in Alaska and off the California coastline, trade operations southwest of that Spanish province, and the very fruitful sandalwood trade between the Sandwich Islands and China."[8]   Known in Hawaiian as *iliahi*, the fragrant sandalwood was used chiefly for perfumes and incense and could be exchanged in China for goods such as tea, china, silks, and nankeen cloth.[9]

In 1815, at the age of 18, Dana traveled with Davis aboard Davis' schooner Eagle to the Sandwich Islands, Alaska, and Canton, among other ports.   During this apprenticeship of sorts, William became an accomplished navigator.   Dana ultimately spent two years in Canton and a year in Calcutta, India.   Richard Pourade, writing about the Boston merchants and sailors who sailed to California in the early 19th century, gives us insight into how Dana may have felt about his stay in China: "Canton was a place to stir any young Puritan from the cold shores of New England.   The river was filled with flower boats with their painted windows and carved in the shape of flowers and birds; mandarin boats with colored silk pennants, and tea-deckers with topsides lacquered in bright colors and with square sails of brown matting.   Thousands of persons lived on the little sampans that choked the river shores.   At night, the light from paper lanterns cast a soft glow over a strange world.   From Canton back to New England was a long way."[10]

* * *

After this extended voyage in the Pacific, Dana returned in 1819 on a "flying trip" to Boston.[11]   There, he renewed old friendships and began a romance with Sarah, a friend of his sister Adeline. A letter written on January 6, 1821, brightly illuminates Sarah's admiration for the young ocean traveler. She begins, "My dear William, You may judge we improve with no small portion of pleasure the opportunity which occurs of writing you – we have been anticipating of ever since your departure for we wished to make you acquainted with family events and while you are buffeting old Neptune inform you how roughly or smoothly we sail down the ocean of time. Well then to commence we have had some adverse winds and tempestuous weather but are at present anchored in a pretty good frost from which I do myself the honor to send you this my journal."[12] Describing her feelings about being separated from William, she continues, "On this day after we set sail from the harbors of separation having passed written communication we touched on the planes of Dejection Disprovidence and Despair at this latter we remained for several successive days, waiting for a suitable breeze to waft us into the channel of anticipation. Favorable winds at length arrived and we were carried almost insensibly into the above mentioned channel and shortly after landed in our present comfortable fort that of Good Hope. Finding this a comfortable haven we have determined to remain here, unless some tidings of dismal import from our fellow Seaman abroad should oblige us to return to the stance of despair."[13] Later, Sarah includes some affectionate teasing about William's appearance. "It is possible William that you may notice a little grease or spots of ink upon the paper ... I think a small portion of grease would benefit your hair, who knows but it might make it darker; I declare if it should, you would be quite a beauty – but perhaps you will not feel inclined to try it, as that would very much increase your debt of gratitude to me. You recollect Adeline always insisted upon it – that she was handsomer than yourself and although you endeavored always to make people believe the reverse, you did not succeed."[14]

The letters of Adeline to her brother reflect her own strong desire to have her brother wed her friend. Initially, her words smack of hope for a possible union. In an early letter she wrote that "Sarah's heart is barricaded against all attacks by an attachment which reflects much honour upon yourself."[15] Dana, however, proved to be a poor correspondent. Upon returning to the Pacific Coast, Dana wrote nary a letter to either Adeline or Sarah. From Hartford, where she was staying with Sarah, Adeline asked him in a letter written in August 1821, "And what is the reason we have not heard from you since your departure?"[16]

HAWAII:
'THE RIGHT SORT OF FELLOW'

Sarah, and the rest of Boston's attractions, clearly had failed to lure Dana back from his new life at sea. Back in the Pacific in 1820, Dana headquartered himself for the next five years in the Sandwich Islands, now called Hawaii. Given title to land on the island of Oahu by King Kamehameha II, Dana established a commercial business and warehouse.[17] Dana's property was located a short distance from Honolulu Harbor in what is now the city's historic district. At the time, his uncle, William Heath Davis, was a prominent member of the American community in Honolulu; however, Davis was criticized by Christian missionaries, many of whom were fellow New Englanders, over "unethical" trading.[18] Davis ultimately died on Oahu in 1822, reportedly of alcoholism.[19] Upon Davis' death, his nephew William received an inheritance of $5,000. The same will granted $5,000 each to Davis' friends Eliab Grimes, John Coffin Jones, and Thomas Meek; $2,000 to John Gowen; and the remainder of Davis' property to Davis' son, Robert G. Davis.[20] Some reports have William using his inheritance to purchase the brigantine Waverly and establish his own trading firm; however, it is more likely that he simply chartered the two-masted vessel, which was owned by King Kamehameha II.[21] The Waverly was of

A brig of the early 1800s

comparable size to other trading ships of the period: 141 tons, 77½ feet long, and 21 feet wide.

From his base in Oahu, Dana focused primarily on trade routes between the Sandwich Islands and California. A list of voyages taken in 1824-1828 includes visits to ports in Kauai, Maui, and Honolulu in the Sandwich Islands; and ports in San Diego, San Pedro, Santa Barbara, Monterey, San Francisco, San Clemente Island, Santa Catalina Island, and the Farallon Islands on the coast of California. Dana also took sealing trips south of Hawaii and as far as Peru. Wrote fellow sea trader Charles Hammatt in a journal, "Yesterday sailed the island Brig Becket ... to day sailed

Island brig Waverly … These vessels are engaged by Dana, the first at 80 or 100 [dollars] p month, & the latter at 800 [dollars], for 6 months to go on a sealing expedition. He will not make any thing, unless he is in a good luck, which I hope he may be, as he is one of the right sort of fellow, such as are not to be picked off from every bush."[22]   Also mentioning Dana was Charles Samuel Stewart, a missionary in Hawaii.   In a March 18, 1824, journal entry recorded from Lahaina, Maui, Stewart writes, "Before I reached home, the Waverly had come to an anchor. Shortly after, Captain [Charles Rand] Smith and Mr. Dana, of Honolulu – who have chartered the brig for a voyage to the Society Islands and New Zealand, called on us; and much to our joy, put into our hands a large packet of letters and papers from America."[23]

Honolulu in the early 1800s

Among Dana's many activities besides sailing was a phosphate mining venture in 1824-25 at Fanning Island, a member of the Line Islands island chain south of Hawaii. The phosphate enterprise failed, however, forcing one of Dana's employees to return to Boston on a whaleship.[24]

* * *

Honolulu, Dana's residence and headquarters, was, in the words of historian Pauline King, "an urban cosmopolitan center for the Hawaiian Kingdom. ... The town was small, extending barely four blocks in from the waterfront and about four blocks paralleling it. Structures were primarily of thatch with wood and stone only gradually being adopted. ... Facilities were primitive, streets dusty or muddy as the weather determined. The population numbered about 3,000 to 4,000 native Hawaiians with more than one hundred foreign residents."[25]   In addition, Honolulu was known for drinking, gambling, and carousing. Resident John Coffin Jones, an acquaintance of Dana in Honolulu, described it as "one of the vilest places on the globe."[26]

A journal kept by friend and business associate Stephen Reynolds affords a revealing glimpse at Dana's life in Hawaii. A fellow American nearly 15 years older than Dana, Reynolds lived with Dana for a time and participated with Dana in the many dinners, parties, and gatherings characteristic of Honolulu during this period. In daily entries kept by Reynolds from 1823 to 1829, Dana is mentioned scores of times. Reynolds began living with Dana on November 20, 1823; in March 1824, he agreed

Stephen Reynolds

with Dana to pay board of $4.00 per week.[27] Most of the entries about Dana are simple recountings of routine landings and business dealings – but many of them show that Dana enjoyed an active life befitting a young man in his late twenties.

When not sailing, trading, or selling, Dana was a prominent participant on the Honolulu social scene. Reynolds' journal is dotted with descriptions of parties, dinners, and *luaus* hosted by Dana, often on Sundays. Dana also owned a billiard room that was popular with fellow foreigners. A sampling of accounts follows: November 24, 1823: "Went up to Mr. Dana's and tarried till near night."[28] Sunday, November 30: "Mr. King took Tea with us at Dana's."[29] December 7, also a Sunday: "Mr. Dana had a party to dine at Wytetee [possibly Waikiki]."[30] December

10: "Mr. Bowman came ashore, went up to Dana's staid till 9 – went to billiard room till 10."[31] December 30: "Mr. Dana gave a dinner to Mr [John Coffin] Jones as he was about to leave the Sandwich Islands – at which Mssrs Goodrich, Ely, & Ruggles were present, among the guests were most of the residents and masters of vessels."[32] Sunday, January 11, 1824: "Mr King, Mr Hunt, Piggins Mr. Johnson (the passenger in Brutus,) Brackett & supped at Dana's."[33] The entry of Tuesday, January 13, is revealing: "Company late at the billiard Room. King & Temple up till ½ past 5 AM. After walking abroad heard among the news of the morning, it was difficult to determine who was farthest gone last evening by pledgeing [sic] to Bacchus. 'He that is without sin – cast the first stone.' Mr Dana gave a dinner, at which were most of the Residents – also the commander of the Russian Brig."[34]

The gregarious Dana hosted his colleagues one to two times per week. Sunday, January 18, 1824: "Attended morning meeting – Noon. Mr. Hammatt and Green dined with mr Dana. Afternoon Mr. Dana – Cap Harris & I went to Wytetee in Whale boat walked up to his house; after, to the village."[35] Monday, February 23: "At 11 went to Mr Dana's to make punch for the guests invited to dine. – Had a fine dinner – a fine time. Evening went to Billiard room, where hot punch was prepared by Mr Dana for those who chose to call – as it had been a jovial day, so it was a jovial meeting in evening."[36] March 6, a Saturday: "Afternoon most of Residents rode to Allens to take punch and melons on invitation of Mr Dana."[37]   Dana is not mentioned in the journal in the second half of 1824 and all of 1825; presumably, he was on the Waverly elsewhere in the Pacific.

Dana's hospitality continued upon his return to Honolulu in early 1826. After arriving in Oahu on January 1, he gave a luau for his friends on Saturday, January 14.[38] Later, on January 17, he "sold his Billiard Room to Weston and others for 700 dollar."[39]   Journal entries for January and February of that year describe Dana hosting another luau, Dana making trips to Pearl River and Waikiki, and the delivery of rum to Dana's house.[40]   On March 13, Dana attended a dinner on board a visiting vessel. "Wind Sd. Capt. McNeill gave a Dinner on board Convoy to Percival and his Officers!! Dana was invited."[41]   Two nights later, Reynolds found himself socializing with Dana. "Evening went up to Dana's with Brooks & the girls to see the magic Lantern [a device with an oil lamp and lens that was a precursor to the modern slide projector]."[42]

Reynolds' writing details the playful side of Dana. On January 3, 1824, Dana won a raffle. "Evening went up to Biliard [sic] room to see the Raffle of two Watches one of which was up at twelve chances at 3 dollars – the other at 1:50 – Mr Dana & Mr Hammatt won the first jointly."[43]   On February 6 of that year, Dana participated in a horse race. "Afternoon a horse-race between Mr Elwell & Mr Dana. Ellwell beat by far."[44]   Later in the journal, on January 16, 1826, Reynolds describes another race involving

Dana. "A race between Dana's & Meeks horses – Dana's for half a mile was a head after Meeks."[45]

Dana's business dealings and expeditions also are described. On December 22, 1823, Dana was "vexed with Temple, & Tibber on account of inattention to their business."[46] February 12, 1824: "Mr. Dana agreed with Pitt for [brig] Inore to go to Island of Guadeloupe [most likely, Guadalupe Island off west coast of Baja California] with sealing party."[47] February 26, 1824: "Got thirteen picul wood from Dana."[48] March 11, 1824: "put 15 yds cloth into Mr Dana's hands to sell in his cruise."[49] September 20, 1824: "Mr Dana in Waverly was at Tahaiti [sic] in July."[50] April 16, 1825: "At 5 Schooner Adonis of Baltimore Cap Sistair fr Tombos and Gallipagos'. Bro't the men from Juan Fernandez [islands off the west coast of Chile] who left Brig Convoy, McNeill – the men from St. Felix whom Dana left there sealing who say they had seven hundred Skins."[51]

* * *

Adeline, in a letter written on December 29, 1825, illustrates the profound contrast between William's life in New England and his new life as a Hawaii-based sea trader. She begins by decrying his absence: "My dear William, I hope this state of privation to which you are subject in your estrangement from your Country and friends, and from so many of the advantages and blessings which a civilized and Christianized state of community would afford you, will soon by over. ... It is indeed hard that my nearest and dearest earthly relationship should be thus laid in desolation by separation. I am sometimes left to wonder that there should be such a necessity for your absence."[52] Later in the letter, she pleads for William's approval for her marriage to a man she has just met (her future husband, Rev. Charles Chauncey Darling, whom she eventually wed in July of 1829).

Adeline also alludes to their Massachusetts relatives' distaste for the mixed-race marriage of William and Adeline's uncle, William Heath Davis. In 1822, just before his death the same year, Davis fathered a child, William Heath Davis Jr. The birth to Hannah Holmes, the daughter of Oliver Holmes of Boston and his Hawaiian wife, caused great upset to Davis' relatives in Boston, most likely because Holmes had Hawaiian ancestry. Describing an aunt's poor health, Adeline writes, "I think her trials in consequence of Uncle William's unmoralities and the disgrace he has entailed upon his family have served more than anything else to crush her spirits and impair her faculties. It has indeed been the means of reducing the family to a state of deep mental suffering. It was an aggravation of the blow too that any proofs of his infamy should be thus publicly brought forward by the transportation of his illegitimate offspring to this country. But the family have never and never will notice the child in any way whatever."[53]

* * *

While willingly accepting a $5,000 inheritance from his uncle, Dana had mixed feelings about another potential inheritance. In 1825, he received documents pertaining to the sale of the ancestral home of his mother in Boston. No great profit was to be realized from the property. Reynolds referred to the situation in a journal entry on June 20, 1826: "Writing to Dana & Copying a power of attorney for him to sign to enable to get an interest in some real Estate – in Boston."[54] In a March 1827 execution of power of attorney for Joshua Davis to sell Dana's interest in the property, Dana expressed misgivings about his right to receive anything from the sale, as he thought the property had been omitted by "mistake from the will of the late Gen. A. Davis, and reverted to the heirs of my grandfather – Robert."[55] He went on, "If I am not one of the rightful heirs, I feel no disposition to retain that which is the property of another contrary to the rules of equity and justice."[56]

During this period, Dana became acquainted with the California coast and was impressed with the business opportunities there. During a visit to Santa Barbara in 1825 he founded a store, leaving it in the hands of Captain Charles Rand Smith. The main customer of Dana's trading post was the mission, which produced "leather hats, coarse woolen cloth, wine from local vineyards, *aguardiente* brandy, and hides and tallow."[57]

Meanwhile, Dana retained his command of the Waverly, continuing his voyages to Canton, Sitka, the Sandwich Islands, other California ports, and elsewhere. Two-masted sailing ships such as the Waverly reportedly were relatively safe, as they "were not large ... and the fewer the sails to handle the less the trouble."[58] An 1826 bill of lading written by Dana lists the cargo aboard the Waverly as including currency, precious metals, and animal skins. "Shipped in good order, and well conditioned, by J.R. Cooper, in and upon the brig called the Waverly, whereof Wm. G. Dana is Master, for this present voyage; now lying in the harbour of St. Barbara, and bound for Oahu, as follows: Fourteen hundred and twenty-eight guilders; two thousand Spanish dollars; four bars silver, weight five hundred and twenty-six marks and five oz., more or less; three casks con'g one hundred and thirty-eight otter skins, more or less; one cask con'g two hundred and twelve black pup fur-seal skins, more or less; and one lump gold, weight unknown, being marked as in the margin (no mark); and are to be delivered in like good order, and well-conditioned, at the aforesaid port of Oahu (the danger of the seas only excepted), unto said Wm. G. Dana, or to S. Reynolds, or their assigns."[59]

* * *

May of 1826 was an eventful month for Dana. It began on May 1 with Dana "landing lumber from Waverly – Selling Deck plank at one dollar each – four or five inches wide – 30 or 40 feet long."[60] On May 9, he transported the native governor Boki to Maui to see Boki's ailing sister. "Dana went to carry Boka up to Mowee to see Waihini-Pio who was sick & sent for him."[61] But Dana apparently left Maui, stranding the governor on the island. On May 15, Reynolds writes, "Yesterday a sail was seen in Pearl River – it proved to be Sch. Young Thaddeus – a Kanaka from here this morning, said they were sent by Boki ... to go to Mauii for him – because W.G. Dana landed Boki and immediately went to Sea!!! it may be true I don't believe it."[62] The next day, Dana "arrived from Mauii. Notwithstanding, *yesterday*, he had Ran off!!"[63]

Also occurring in May was Dana's detainment by British Naval Captain Frederick W. Beechey, whose ship HMS Blossom was anchored in Honolulu en route to a surveying expedition in the Bering Strait. Reynolds' May 24 entry reads as follows: "afternoon Waverly went out – Capt Beechy Fired a gun at the Waverly – hailed and ordered him, Dana, to come on board with the papers – demanded to know why he did not pay the men, he had discharged, the wages due them. Sent Dana ashore for papers, with Sergeant to be Sentry over him. The late & present Naval Commanders seem to assume a great power to themselves – by overhauling & stopping the vessels at Anchor & passing out of the Harbor. An English sailor had said that Dana owed him fifteen dollars, when it appeared Dana had orders for more than fifty-dollars."[64] The next day, Beechey allowed Dana to "go to Sea, as the papers shewn [sic] were satisfactory."[65] The month concluded with Dana having difficulty commencing a planned voyage. On May 29, "Dana preparing to get off in heaving up his chain parted & he lost his Anchor & fourteen fathoms of chain. bo't one of Spurr – at Sunset he put off – it grew dark so fast he could not find the vessel – he returned & Slept all night. ... Dana agreed with a particular young lady to wait for him at his return."[66]   Dana successfully launched his brig on May 30.

In January 1827, Dana landed in Hawaii from Santa Barbara. Reynolds describes a sequence of landing, selling, and trading that typifies the maritime dealings of the day. He also reveals what Hawaiians would have heard about California and exploration in the West. January 28: "Very strong Trades. Brig Waverly arrived 15 days from St Barbara – cargo – Horses – Sheep & a Calf – confirms the News that Capt. [John Rogers] Cooper will lose all he has earned Said a Mr. [Jedediah] Smith had been at California, having crossed the Rocky Mountains and arrived at St Gabriel had left and gone to Columbia River!! That posts have been established all the way from St Louis to Co'a River That trade is dull on the Coast of California."[67] January 29: Several of officers visited us to day – for trade. Bo't a colt of Dana, & a calf Sent colt to Allen's – Dana took house for his goods."[68]   January 30: "Dana Landing goods. Temple [John Temple, a business partner of Dana's] opening Store."[69] January 31: "Mr. Dana Selling quite lively & Brisk."[70]

On February 16, Dana had another encounter with Captain Beechey of the Royal Navy. "Mr Charlton getting information about a man of Mr Dana's who went on board Blossom and entered complaint to Capt Beechey, that Dana would not pay him his wages, when it appears the man was in Capt Dana's Debt."[71]

* * *

In 1827, Dana made a commitment to California. He decided to forsake Oahu and establish permanent residence in the province, in the port city of Santa Barbara. A principal reason for the move likely was the decline of the heretofore-prosperous sandalwood trade. By 1827, Hawaii's sandalwood forests had been depleted to such an extent that the slow-growing tree was nearly eradicated; accordingly, the economy of Oahu suffered greatly.

Dana closed out his affairs in the Islands, leaving his property there in the hands of associate Stephen Reynolds. On March 7, 1827, he and his partner John Temple shuttered their store in Honolulu. Writes Reynolds, "Dana & Temple gave up the Store. Understood Mr Dana had given orders to have a large house built!! another building in Santa Barbara!!! Something else at St Diego."[72] Dana, obviously intending to leave for California, threw a large party on Saturday, May 19 – two days after his 30th birthday. "W.G. Dana gave a Dinner to all the people he could find, amounting to fifteen at Mr Knight's."[73] On Thursday, May 24, Dana set sail. Writes Reynolds, "Fine morn – Mr Dana started early in morning having slept with his Dearie – the last night."[74]

Research done by Thomas Wheeler shows that the "Dearie" to whom Reynolds referred may have been either the mother of Dana's child or Dana's wife. The key to Wheeler's findings are Hawaiian records of testimony regarding an 1847 dispute over land Dana owned in Honolulu. One claimant to Dana's quarter-acre Lot 644 (located on

Alakea Street in what is now Honolulu's Chinatown) was a man named William Dany, who purports to be Dana's son. Dany's letter of August 24, 1847, to the Hawaiian land commissioners includes the following: "I herby [sic] petition you to act on my claim to houselot. ... My lot is from my *makuakane* [father], it is an old right, because my *makuakane* lived here a very long time. My *makuakane* and my *makuahine* [mother] were living at this place before Liholiho [King Kamehameha II] sailed for England, and I lived there in my childhood. We left that place until the time my *makuakane* sailed for Spain [presumably meaning California here], then I and my *makuahines* lived at that place."[75] Dany, who would have been in his 20s at the time, goes on to say the lot wound up in the hands of a relative named "I", who sought to give the land to her older sister. He concludes, "It is for you to investigate this. This right is not for 'I' but for my *makuakane*, William Dany, and I am his son and heir. I have many witnesses as to this. With aloha, William Dany."[76]

Testimonials by other parties depict a circumstance in which Dana fathered a child by one Hawaiian woman and later married the woman's sister. Writes a man named Nuuanu: "Claimant [Dany] got this place from his father, who is now at California. I am stepfather to Cl. Claimant's mother Ii acknowledged the land do be his at her death and ordered me to live under him. Which I have done to this time."[77] Offers a man named Levi: "I know the boundaries are true which have been given, and that claimant got the land from his father who is in California. I heard the lad spoken of; but I heard Claimants mother say she had given the land to him. Cap: Daney owned the land in time of Boki of whom he bought it."[78] Attests Pulehu, a counterclaimant to the lot, "All belonged to the wife of William Dana, father of W. Dana Smith [Dany appears to have gone by this name as well] the constable. William Dana received it from the King Rihoriho [King Kamehameha II]; and when he left the island he gave this place to 'I' his wife. … 'I' was not the mother of William Dana Smith."[79]

Two more witnesses describe how Dana intended for his son William to inherit the parcel. Says Kalenkule: "I know this place it belongs to W.D. Smith. I lived on it when his father was living there. His name was William Daney. Liholiho gave him the land. I helped him to fence it. His wife's name was 'I'. He went away when his son William was a little boy. 'I' was his mother's sister; and his father put the land into her keeping. I went to California with his father and when I left him he said to me "Tell 'I' my wife to take care of that place for my son William. That he may have it when he grows up!! Meaning this place. I told her what he said and she kept it until her death for him as I understood."[80] Swore Kaneuhapa, backing Kalenkule's story: "Many years since when Kalenkule returned from California where he went with William Daney, I heard my sister say that she heard him tell 'I' the foster mother of his son William, that he had sent word to her to take care of the child and his land for him; and upon that I gave up

William who was living with me to 'I' to take care of. I heard her give this place in 1840 to William. She said she willed it to him."[81]

Other information about the connections between Dana, the two women, and the man named William Dany may reside in Hawaii. Present and future scholars doubtless will seek to uncover more about this episode in his life.

SANTA BARBARA:
'SETTLING IN THE DAMN'D COUNTRY'

Dana continued to captain the Waverly until July 1827, when he "took leave of the ship and left [first officer Thomas] Robbins in command."[82]   Dana apparently felt it would greatly simplify his business relations with Californians to live in California, embrace the Catholic faith, and apply for naturalization as a citizen of Mexico. Accordingly, Rev. Father Antonio Menendez, chaplain of the Presidio of San Diego, "reconciled to holy Mother Church and baptized, after adequate instruction," Dana on July 29, 1827.[83]   Dana filed his petition for naturalization by February 1828.

Dana's choice of Santa Barbara was a logical one. Dana's distant cousin Richard Henry Dana, who visited the area in the mid-1830s, said the town was "finely situated, with a bay in front, and an amphitheater of hills behind."[84] The famed traveler Sir George Simpson observed some years later in comparing it to another California town, "Santa Barbara, in many respects, being to Monterey what the parlor is to the kitchen."[85]

* * *

Despite the new opportunities, Dana's early years in California were a time of adjustment and frustration. His letters to friend and fellow New England emigrant John

Rogers Cooper reflect both his disgust with the Mexican institutions that delayed his marriage and his impatience with the business climate in Mexican California. The writings depict a man who, while determined to make a place for himself in California, nonetheless preferred Yankee ways to those of the Mexicans who ruled the territory. The correspondence between Dana and Cooper also can be considered among the more candid and entertaining exchanges in the history of early California.

Dana valued his friendship with someone who had similar experiences in life and in California. Six years older than Dana, Cooper was born in England and had a childhood similar to Dana's. Early in his life, Cooper's father was lost at sea, and his widowed mother subsequently brought nine-year-old John to Boston.[86] Like Dana, Cooper became a ship's captain who sailed around the Horn to Pacific ports in China, California, the Sandwich Islands, South America, and elsewhere.[87] Like Dana, Cooper had spent time in Honolulu; in fact, the two men became acquainted with each other there. Like Dana, Cooper established a successful trading business and store – only in Cooper's case he chose to settle in Monterey. Like Dana, Cooper married a younger Mexican woman; in August of 1827, he wed Encarnacion Vallejo, sister of future General Mariano Vallejo.[88]

Dana plainly relished the opportunity to share thoughts and views with his friend, and he wrote quite candidly about them. In one letter, dated January 5, 1827,

John Rogers Cooper

he bemoaned his medical regimen for digestive problems. "I am now in a hell of a stew being under the operation of a double dose of Calomel [a derivative of mercury used at the time to relieve constipation] ... taken last night. ... In haste, Wm. G. Dana."[89]   In a letter dated November 6, 1827, Dana chastised Cooper for letting his marriage interfere with their correspondence. "I am apt to think," he wrote, "that matrimony does not agree with you that in lieu of enlivening your spirits it makes you as dull as the fat weed ... which rots itself with motion, else why this long silence – here am I obliged to get all my news second hand? ... I heard of your marriage a fortnight before it had taken place."[90]

Dana himself had apparently been pondering the issue of marriage. In the same November 6 letter, Dana wondered about the apparent effortlessness of Cooper's union: "I also learn that they have passed a law prohibiting the marriage of foreigners in the country unless naturalized – pray how did you get over this difficulty – did you gulp down baths of allegiance?"[91] Later in the letter, Dana mused about his own prospects, claiming that he was the object of a government grudge. "I shall certainly learn <u>something</u> in California, for I never knew before that in issuing <u>general orders</u> it was necessary to <u>specify persons</u> but I find in the order to prevent the marriage of foreigners particular mention is made of Don <u>Guillermo G. Dana</u> … I am coming to Monterey to conclude my matrimonial scheme either <u>one</u> way or <u>the other</u> and in the mean time shall set my heart to the tune of 'sacks alive.'"[92]

* * *

Dana's letters to Cooper fulminate about the delay imposed by the Mexican government on Dana's own marriage. In a petition dated March 22, 1828, Dana asked the governor of California, General Jose Maria de Echeandia, for permission to marry at once Maria Josefa Carrillo, daughter of one of Santa Barbara's most prominent citizens, Carlos Antonio Carrillo. The Carrillos were related to several other leading California families, including the Bandini, Lugo, de la Guerra, and Ortega families. Carrillo's wife, Maria Josefa Castro, was the sister of General Jose Castro, the military commander of California. Despite these connections, the governor replied, in a letter dated May 1, that Dana's application for marriage could not be approved for five months, at which time Dana's papers of naturalization would be processed.

Dana's discouragement about the lengthy wait for his wedding is evident in a letter to Cooper written after Echeandia answered his application for marriage. In a sarcastic note penned on May 12, 1828, he wrote, "My affairs with the good folks at the head of the administration remain in status quo. They are determined to bother me all they can and vice versa. … I have learned just enough Spanish to get my head broke."[93] He concluded the note, however, with praise for his fiancée: "If she had shown the least disposition to retract I should have been off long ago but am now determined to carry it through thick and thin."[94] Dana's gloomy mood carried through into a letter written July 13. "As regards my marriage," he said, "there is

Carlos Antonio Carrillo

as little probability as ever. Don Carlos [future father-in-law Carrillo] has written to the <u>Great Man</u> upon the subject and received for answer that he would let him know by next post – but the next post came without any communication whatever, as usual with his promises. Hereabouts all is confusion – but I get along in the crowd about as well as any."[95]

Cooper, for his part, was indignant over the treatment given Dana by the government. In a letter written to Dana on July 22, 1828, a homesick Cooper excoriated California culture. "There is not one jot of honesty, truth, honor, or principle in the country, but a set of the most shameless, swindling, deceitful rascals that ever dwelt on earth. Oh! 'Home,' Dana, 'sweet, sweet home, there is no place like

Maria Josefa Carrillo Dana

home.'"[96]   In the same letter Cooper, the older half-brother of future United States Consul Thomas O. Larkin, expressed the hope that the United States would eventually conquer California. "This country, I fear, will never do for you nor me. The only hope I have is that they will kick up a dust with the United States and we may have a different Government here."[97]   In a letter written in the same period to his friend James Hunnewell, Cooper expressed an opinion that Dana may well have shared. "When I think of home," said Cooper, "I wish to God I was in Boston again … for I have set my hat against these people [who] are trying every restriction on foreigners in this country to their own injury and ruining the trade here entirely."[98]

* * *

Marriage to a native daughter was not required by law. Such an alliance, however, served to demonstrate an American's sincere intention to remain in California. Dana opted to obey Echeandia's order, but not without considerable frustration. After waiting the required five months from March, the 31-year-old Dana and the 16-year-old Carrillo were married at Mission Santa Barbara on August 20, 1828. The official record lists as witnesses Joaquin Maitorena, the commander of the Presidio, and Maitorena's wife, Ysabel.[99]

One of Dana's sons, Juan Francisco Dana, later wrote about what he thought happened with his parents' marriage. "It may have been on that first trip [in 1825, when Dana opened a store in Santa Barbara] that he met my Spanish mother," he said. "But from stories handed down in our family, it was not until 1828 that my father wooed and won my mother. Five long months of that year he waited until the 'American hater,' Governor … Echeandia granted the necessary permission. … Whether they were married at the presidio or the mission, I do not know but marriages were celebrated on a grand scale in those days and the festivities probably lasted for days."[100] He added that another American emigrant, Captain Henry Fitch, and his wife eloped to Chile when confronted with Echeandia's hostility.[101]

The news of William and Maria Josefa's nuptials traveled overseas and across the continent. Stephen Reynolds' journal entry of September 12, 1828, includes mention of the wedding. "De Chille arrived from St Diego, 17 Days. Mr Dana was married August 23."[102]   By late 1828, Dana's sibling Adeline, who had not heard from her brother for "nearly two years," had learned of Dana's decision to stay in California and marry there.[103]   In a November 23 letter, she wrote, "I was very much astonished that you did not write me a line. ... and that I should receive through so cold a medium [a Captain Meek had told her], information so nearly concerning your happiness. I congratulate you with heartfelt sincerity on any events in your life which may promote your happiness – though they destroy some of my own anticipations [referring to her hopes for a union between Sarah and William]. It is painful to me to think that you are permanently locating in a foreign land – that you are there forming interests which will probably detain you there for life."[104]

The span in years between husband and wife was common with American settlers. Dana's friend Cooper was 36 and his bride Encarnacion Vallejo 18 when they married in 1827[105]; another Dana friend, William Foxen, was 34 when he married 19-year-old Eduarda del Carmen Osuna in 1831.[106]   Interestingly, Maria Josefa established a family precedent by marrying a Yankee, as each of her sisters followed suit in the years to follow. Encarnacion Carrillo married Thomas Robbins, a first officer of Dana's who ultimately was granted title to Catalina Island. Francisca Carrillo married Alpheus Thompson, recipient of a land grant covering both sides of the Stanislaus River

William Foxen

near the base of the Sierra mountains. Manuela Carrillo married John Coffin Jones, who later was given partial title to Santa Rosa Island along with his brother-in-law Thompson. Maria Antonia Carrillo married Luis Trumbull Burton, who was granted Rancho Jesus Maria, which lies within present-day Vandenberg Air Force Base. William and Maria Josefa were official witnesses at the respective weddings of Maria's brother Jose, her sister Francisca, and her sister Encarnacion.

The path taken by Dana in marrying a native Californian is aptly captured in advice given by Daniel Hill to Dr. Nicholas A. Den: "You must become a Mexican in heart, soul, and body, not in name only. Your future wife will probably speak only Spanish. You must adopt her language, not insist that she speak English. This is a Mexican *provincia*, remember, and except for occasional Yankee trading schooners, you will rarely get an opportunity to use your English anyway. Before you know it you'll speak it with an accent."[107]

* * *

Dana's letters to Cooper also display his discontent with the business environment in California. A victim of faulty money-lending decisions, he told Cooper about the welshing of California businessmen. Speaking of a shipment of hides and tallow in a letter dated May 12, 1828, he wrote, "I will try and muster funds to take it up, but to tell you the truth I am also damn'd hard push'd as it is all outpour and no income and I expect to lose a thousand Dollars in bad Debts on the lower part of the coast. … I will be glad if at the end of the season I can make both ends meet."[108] In his letter of July 13, he said, "I like a damn'd fool have been buying every thing that came along and now expect to have to scrape hell to pay Rodgers and a balance of about two thousand to the Courier although I have above eighty thousand dollars due me in the damn'd country and would willingly take five for the whole but I am determined that every one that does not pay by November to sue. I have almost given up all idea of settling in the damn'd country."[109]

More of Dana's discouragement can be found in later letters. On October 28, 1828, he wrote, "I have had damn'd bad luck as regards my debts and expect to lose at least two thousand dollars in San Diego alone. I have been able to meet all my debts as they come in and hope I shall still be able to but I will see the whole of the Coast of California damn'd before I trust them again as I have done. If you wish to make a man your enemy in this country do him a favor by lending him a couple of hundred dollars."[110] Business apparently had not improved by 1830. Writing from Santa Barbara on June 25 of that year, Dana told Cooper, "I have shipp'd on bard [sic] Brig <u>Plant</u> and consign'd to you, six boxes of soap cont'g 3,200 cakes in order to try the market of Monterey, and if answers I can from time to time supply you with most any quantity as I intend to turn <u>soap boiler</u> for a livlihood [sic]. There is no business of any name or nature down this way and I am about discouraged, though to discourage me is no easy matter."[111]

During this time, Dana continued to correspond with his business associates in Hawaii. Stephen Reynolds, on February 9, 1829, "recd. Letters from Dana, saying Waverly would be here in a month or two, with funds to me, and a horse."[112] The next day, Reynolds was given "a Cask containing thirty Sea Otter Skins belonging to W.G. Dana."[113] On April 1, Reynolds divided or sold the property Dana had left on Hawaii. "Afternoon Divided Dana's horse with Boki [the Hawaiian governor]. 19 in number Sold most of my lot. Sold Mr French a lot of Sea-otter skins belonging to Dana & Temple – primes at 35.00 Small at 12.00 – Reds at 5.00, pieces of tails 1.00 each."[114] April 16: "Sold a quantity clothing to Boki to pay off the crew of Waverly – also to pay balance of crew with Dana."[115]

The situation in California improved for Dana and Cooper. Though both criticized Mexican ways in their correspondence, the fact is that, lacking an alternative to the existing government, both adjusted to it. They and many of their Yankee counterparts lived prosperously under Mexican rule. Dana, Cooper, and others adopted Catholicism, took out Mexican citizenship, and received large land grants and the wealth springing therefrom. William Goodwin became Guillermo G. Dana, and John Rogers became Juan Bautista Rogers Cooper. As they worked to make a place for themselves in California, the "sweet home" of the East took position in the back of their minds.

Santa Barbara:
'Business on Hand'

Dana's aspirations for an American conquest of California were forgotten as he was drawn progressively deeper into his California life. His correspondence with the trader Abel Stearns of Los Angeles reflects the attention he gave to his store and to public service in the *pueblo* of Santa Barbara. Dana's letters to Stearns take a more neutral perspective on life in California than his letters to John Rogers Cooper; nevertheless, they are quite valuable in shedding light on Dana's transition from Yankee to Californian.

Like Cooper, Stearns bore many similarities to Dana. Born in Lunenberg, Massachusetts, a year after Dana, Stearns was orphaned at the age of 12 and went to sea, where he traveled the trade routes to China, South America, and California. At the age of 30, he decided to settle in Mexico to "seek his fortune."[116] He became naturalized as a Mexican, and ultimately ended up in California, where in 1829 he established a store in Los Angeles. After differences with the Mexican governor during which he was ordered out of the territory from 1831-1834, Stearns re-established himself by purchasing a warehouse that had been used by Mission San Gabriel to keep hides. With the warehouse as central storage for hides, Stearns bartered groceries, dry

Abel Stearns

goods, and liquor for hides and tallow – which he then sold
to sea captains from the United States.[117]   Stearns' papers,
which include several letters from Dana, illustrate "the
thriving business [Stearns] developed by inserting himself
between the *rancheros* and the Yankee traders. He made a
small fortune in this enterprise."[118]

Most of Dana's correspondence with Stearns show
one businessman working deals with another. On April 1,
1833, Dana shares some information regarding his father-
in-law Carrillo and his friend Cooper. "I ... send you
Carrillo's bill, which is not so much as I suppos'd. ... Juan
Bautista will deliver you one hundred & eighteen hides and

more if possible."[119]   Later in the letter, he discusses an effort to provide help to a friend. "Tell [word unreadable] I did not send his mule from Ranch as I heard of the arrival of a boat from the Island and thought I might get him a Kanaka [Hawaiian native].[120]   One has partly agreed to go and if he makes up his mind I shall send him down in course of the week. I shall also send him the traps & the cottons he ask'd for by Roxana."[121]   At the end of the letter, Dana gives Stearns some advice: "For mercy's sake collect all you can and start for the Beach as fast as possible – California sails day after tomorrow."[122]   On December 17, 1838, Dana makes a humble request. "Do me the favor to let the Bearer of this Give H la Paz [half] the amount of twenty one dollars in goods from your store and I will pay the same to you credit – in % with Mr. Thompson. He brot [sic] an order on me for the [amount] and an order at the same time for the Hides to pay the [amount] but as I have no goods of any kind in the store except molasses and tea – I hope that the poor fellow might not be disappointed."[123]

In his correspondence with Stearns, Dana often included news that he had heard from the region. In an undated letter, he laments various rumors and reports: "On my Journey from the Pueblo to this place I heard a variety of reports which rais'd my dander a little but since my arrival I can find no one to Father them they having been rais'd by Mr. Ninguno. … Sancho's time I believe is about up & hope you have been able to drum up a few new things among the rest as regards the variety of reports in circulation in the Pueblo you may set down nineteen [word unreadable] of them for damn'd lies & without an author."[124]   Later in the same letter, Dana brings up a man named Aguirre, possibly the sea trader Jose Antonio Aguirre: "Aguirre has a damn'd right to say about it and lays it all to foreigners. In fact reports say he lets his tongue 'wag rather' to [sic] much – more than I expect would be safe for him in the Pueblo."[125]   In an 1836 letter, Dana updates Stearns on an incident in Monterey: "I have no news but what you probably have heard of on the Rumpus in Monterey where the inhabitants rose and [word unreadable] all Mexicans out of employ except Don Angel."[126]   Another 1836 letter contains a description of a leader who may have been a governor at the time: "Our much respected and dearly belov'd recent Commander in Chief has just arriv'd in this place in the Clementine on his papage [voyage] to other side. He remains on board and he will not trust himself among the Barbarians and I am sorry to inform you that you have lost your papage by not being ready. I have not yet waited on the Cavallero but tomorrow shall go on board to congratulate him in regenerating California."[127]

Dana's letters also included the latest on events elsewhere in the world. On July 7, 1836, Dana wrote of a friend who landed in Santa Barbara aboard the schooner Dolphin, "direct from Acapulco – he brings news that Gen'l Sta Ana drove the inhabitants of Texas before him and had almost completed the conquest – but by some accident or other was taken Prisoner with about sixty of his principal officers, his troops without a leader have return'd to Mexico and the Country in a state of great commotion trying to raise an army to attempt his recapture – so much for Mexican news."[128]   Later in the letter, Dana discusses Peru: "Peru is in a terrible state – Anderson has again come out and it is more than probable will be on this coast. The Row between France and the United States is settled at last."[129]   He ends the same letter with a brief quip to Stearns underneath his signature: "No doubt you will be <u>sorry</u> to hear of Sta Ana's capture."[130]

* * *

During the years in which Dana carried on his communication with Stearns, he also was becoming involved in local politics. Dana, though a strident critic of the Mexican government, ironically ended up serving it in several positions. Among his political offices were appraiser at La Purisima Mission, captain of the port of Santa Barbara, and alcalde (mayor and judge) of Santa Barbara in 1836. The role of "captain of the port" was especially significant, as Dana was "responsible for collection of port fees, duties, and compilation of shipping records."[131]   Dana may have been aided in his political involvement in Santa Barbara by his marriage into the Carrillo family. Carlos Carrillo was a man of influence in the region who was allied, through the marriage of his sister, to the powerful de la Guerra family.

In a February 27, 1836, letter to Stearns, Dana described his election as alcalde with his usual mix of candor, humility, and humor. "You have doubtless heard before this that the good folks of this vicenity [sic] have thought that I had not botheration enough of my own and therefore have thought people to elect me to the unwished and unthankful office of Alcalde – I was about taking a Trip to the Pueblo when it took place but now cannot leave till I get a permit from the *Gefe Politico*. I have sent for permission to help to the great City and expect to receive permission by Mr. Burk in course of three or four days."[132] In the body of the letter, he commented on being alcalde: "I have been trying here to make folks pay their debts but have not yet try'd to recover any of my own as my time has been mostly spent battling the watch with Administrators & the Military."[133]

Dana also related the story of how two elections were needed to confirm him in the public office. "The [first] Election was declar'd null & of no effect under the plea that the Electors were not sufficient in number being but nine … On the second Election I had the whole of the votes so there could be no mistake. I believe it did not give great satisfaction to the folks of the bighouse but very little did I care about that and although I had rather have been excus'd from an office that will interfere so much with my business but it is some gratificacion [sic] to see that it is by the gen'l wish of the Pueblo."[134]   Later, on March 4, 1836, Dana described public service with his usual wit. "I am up to my a-s in business doing nothing but settling the afairs [sic] of the Public and neglecting my own; but it would not be so bad if I had not so much damn'd Ignorance to contend with for you know you can deal [word unreadable] with three

Rogues than one fool. But I've lot of business on hand & shall only say Chin Chin, Guillermo G. Dana."[135]

The letters to Stearns from Dana rarely mention any longing for home. The only reference to life in the United States is contained in a description of Santa Barbara: "Nothing new here – everything dull as State Life – all waiting new arrivals – & brisker times for which fervantly [sic] prays."[136] Dana's communication to his fellow storeowner Stearns, while not as revealing as his letters to Cooper, does show how immersed he was in the affairs – business and public – of his new hometown.[137]

* * *

As Dana was running a store, he also was capitalizing on the lucrative otter-hunting business. Not only was it profitable, with otter pelts being sold for as much as $2,500 each to Chinese customers, it also afforded him the companionship of fellow Yankee emigrants to California.[138] Ironically, the otter trade, which lured many Americans to California, declined just as the United States was winning control of the territory.

Dana, like his friend John Rogers Cooper, profited from his license by sending others to sea rather than going hunting himself. In the 1820s, he became interested in the California otter trade. Dana's naturalization in 1828 made him eligible to receive a hunting license, and in 1830 he obtained one to operate 10 boats for hunting sea otter between San Luis Obispo and Bodega. At that time he was "the first foreigner" to hold such a license from the Mexican

Otter hunters displaying pelts

government.[139]   Dana's main source of revenue came from
the letting out of his permit to American hunters who could
not obtain such a license. In exchange for the use of Dana's
license and for provisions, hunters gave Dana 40 percent of
their catch. Among those hunting under Dana's hire were
George Nidever, Isaac Galbraith, George C. Yount, Lewis
T. Burton, Isaac Sparks, Allen Light, and Daniel Sill.

One of the otter hunters employed by Dana was
the expert marksman Isaac Galbraith. Hunting from Santa
Rosa Island, part of the Santa Barbara Channel Islands
group, Galbraith and two Kanakas (Hawaiian natives)
brought in as many as 30 otters a week.[140]   "From the shore
he [Galbraith] shot into their midst, his Kanaka swimmers
bringing in the slaughtered game."[141]   By 1831, Dana had
invested in "otter boats" which sailed out of Santa Barbara
on hunting expeditions. Galbraith, however, only hunted
for Dana for a short while, as "he chafed at doing all the
work and getting only half the spoils."[142]

To replace Galbraith, Dana sought out the trapper George C. Yount, a rough-hewn North Carolina native who had come West with the William Wolfskill party in 1831. Though Yount's "strange apparel and perfectly unique appearance excited some attention and made him a subject of notoriety," satisfactory terms were arranged between the two at a meeting in Santa Barbara.[143] Dana, for half of the proceeds, would furnish provisions, canoes, and transportation to the Channel Islands or coast, and Yount and his helpers would receive the other half. Yount and Dana got along well, Yount becoming "the favorite of the master mariner with whom he sailed."[144] Dana even paid Yount a one-dollar-a-day fee during the off-season in order to retain the trapper's services.[145]

George Nidever, also a trapper, was employed by Dana as an otter hunter in 1835-36. Nidever later described the Santa Barbara scene in mid-1835: "At that time it was impossible for newcomers to procure a license. Capt. Denny [Dana], the Capt. Of this port, had a license, and Burton, Sparks and other hunters then here hunted under his license, paying him a share of the skins."[146] Nidever, who said he hunted under Dana's license "for about a year and a half or two years," wrote about an otter expedition up the coast in late 1835 with Allen Light, an African-American otter hunter also known by his nickname "Black Steward": "We went as far up as San Luis Obispo, were gone 3 or 4 months, and got 50 otter skins. We paid Capt. Denny 40% of our skins; he furnishing our provisions and paying the wages of one man for each hunter."[147] Nidever's last trip under Dana's permit took place in late April or early May of 1836. "Black Steward and I continued up the coast," he wrote, "and did not return until Nov. following. We got about 60 skins."[148] Nidever later sought Dana's assistance in an unsuccessful effort to secure a Mexican land grant in San Luis Obispo County.[149]

As Dana was assimilating and becoming Mexican, he was using his newfound status to help his fellow Yankee emigrants. One of the conditions of receiving a license was that native Californians were to comprise two-thirds of a hunting crew. It was apparent, however, that "Dana's parties were never known to fulfill the law in this respect."[150] Dana also helped the famous fur trapper and explorer Jedediah Strong Smith clear himself from the suspicion of Echeandia's Mexican government. Smith, trying to refute the accusation that he or any of his band were an expeditionary force representing the American government, obtained a document attested to by such American shipmasters as Dana, William N. Cunningham, and William Henderson. Dana's first officer, Thomas Robbins, also signed the document. The document, which was presented to Echeandia on December 20, 1826, stated that Smith was interested only in the "hunting and trapping of beaver, and other furs."[151]

The otter trade declined in the late 1840s, but not before encouraging many Americans to establish themselves permanently in California. Dana "dealt in otter ... up until about 1848 when the animals were about wiped out from years of forays from the Aleutian Islands and every other point. ... It was during the later days of the Mexican period when the Russians brought so many Aleut hunters down from Alaska that otter hunting was the 'biggest thing' on the coast. ... But the Russians eventually wiped out that industry here."[152]

* * *

An upshot of the otter trade was Dana's historical building of a schooner in 1828. Realizing the need for a ship for otter hunting and for coastal shipping, Dana headed the construction, at "a great deal of expense", of a 33-ton ship off the coast of Santa Barbara, near the present city of Goleta.[153] The shipyard was on the Atascadero Inlet, which is connected to the Goleta Estuary.[154] The building of the schooner was a collaborative effort, as Dana was joined by his father-in-law Carlos Carrillo and his friend William Foxen. In fashioning the boat, the men utilized the metal fittings of a damaged ship, Danube: "the planking of the hull, the knees and a lot of the iron, brass, copper cleats, and fastenings."[155] The Danube had been wrecked near what is today San Pedro, and Dana purchased the remnants. Wrote Danube co-owner William Hartnell, who sold Dana the fittings, "Yesterday the Hull as it lies stripped of everything was knocked off to Dana for 425 dollars, who also afterwards bought the spars, rigging, probably the whole cost will be about $2,000."[156] Dana had salvaged the parts from damaged ships before; in Hawaii, he had taken copper and iron from a shipwreck.[157] Pine timber "brought from the San Marcos by the Indians" was used for the mast and keel of the schooner.[158]

As with his marriage, Dana faced obstacles from Echeandia's Mexican bureaucracy in licensing his schooner for trade. He wrote Cooper on June 20, 1829, about the problem: "My cutter is launch'd and they are now rigging her after every possible impediment from the Gen'l, which cost the old man a jaunt to San Diego. I am again at hammer and tongs with the good folks about letters of naturalization – as by the law I am entitled to them."[159]

After a number of delays, Dana finally received the desired license, but not before encountering more resistance from the government in the form of a condition that Jose Carrillo be the captain and at least half of the six-man crew be Mexican. Dana named the schooner La Fama and relied on it for his trade with the Sandwich Islands. "My father often told me that the schooner was a first-class ship for its day and had a capacity of eighty-three tons," said Juan Francisco. "She ... was used by my father for several years."[160]

According to many sources, the schooner was the first ship ever put together in California. "There is a belief that Jose Chapman built a ship for the padres of San Gabriel somewhere in 1826," writes Juan Francisco, "but no documents have ever proved it, so it looks as if Captain Dana built the first homemade ship in California on Santa Barbara's coast."[161] Regardless of its position in the annals of California history, the vessel lasted a long time. In later years it was sold and renamed the <u>Santa Barbara</u>. In 1846 it was purchased by Daniel Hill, who owned a land grant where present-day Goleta is. Hill renamed the ship <u>La Goleta</u> in honor of the spot where it was launched. The ship reportedly was sold for the last time in Acapulco.[162]

William Goodwin Dana

'THE PLACE NAMED NIPOMO'

Not quite a year after their wedding, Dana and his bride Maria Josefa started their family. On July 9, 1829, a daughter, Maria Josefa, was born. A son was born nearly a year later, and in a letter to Cooper written June 25, 1830, Dana discussed the birth of his second child: "My wife was brought to bear the ninth of June of a Son which died next night – but if she breeds so fast – we will soon have enough – it being eleven months to a day from the birth of the son – that being born the ninth of July last year."[163]   Four more children died in infancy before a son, William Charles, was able to survive and live a normal life. The Danas eventually had 21 children, 13 of whom lived to adulthood.[164]   No twins were born, so Maria Josefa had 21 single births dating from July of 1829, when she was 17, to April of 1855, when she was 42. The first 16 were born in Santa Barbara; the rest were born at the family's home in Nipomo.

Meanwhile, Dana was becoming intrigued by the possibility of gaining a land grant from the Mexican government. The generous tracts of land available after the secularization of the missions attracted not only native Californians but the few Yankees living in the province at the time. Such American-born residents as Dana were eligible to receive ranchos of great size at little expense.

Land was such an important issue for Dana that it loomed large in his mind as early as 1829. In a letter written on June 20 to his friend John Rogers Cooper, Dana said, "I leave this day for San Gabrail [sic], to get [word torn from paper] for our farm (what by the way I forgot to tell you we have got a fine one) – capable of rearing five thousand head and plenty of wood, water and planting ground."[165] While it is not known which parcel Dana was referring to in that letter, it is known that Dana spent time at Rancho Sespe, a land grant owned by his father-in-law Carlos Antonio Carrillo. The 8,800-acre rancho was located east of Ventura, between present-day Santa Paula and Fillmore and along the Santa Clara River. As per a partnership with his father-in-law, Dana was assigned to oversee the cattle on the land during a trip by Carrillo to Mexico in 1831-1832; as a dividend, Dana would receive half of the cattle upon Carrillo's return. Carrillo's stay in Mexico was consequential; he spoke to the Mexican National Congress on October 18, 1831, in a successful effort to remove military law in California in favor of establishing civil courts "for the administration of justice."[166]

When Carrillo came back from Mexico, Dana received at least 500 head of cattle, and possibly many more.[167] In 1835, Dana petitioned in his wife's name for a land grant in the Ojai Valley. When no action was taken, he inquired about the Corral de Piedra *rancho* just south of San Luis Obispo. Juan Francisco Dana later recalled that his father was denied the Corral property because the "mission padres" said they needed it as "pasturing ground" for the mission cattle.[168]   During this time, Dana and his family were living in a house in Santa Barbara located adjacent to the Presidio.[169]

* * *

Dana turned his attention to Nipomo, a large piece of land located approximately 60 miles northwest of Santa Barbara. The name "Nipomo" derives from the Chumash Indian word "ne-po-mah," which meant "foot of the hill." The April 14, 1835, application Dana composed to the governor was written with deference and his characteristic descriptiveness: "Guillermo Dana, a native of Boston, in the United States of North America, naturalized in this Territory, and married with a woman of this country, before Your Honor, with due respect represent; That my wife, having made a petition about a year since for the place named Ojay [sic] … and having learned … that, there are other petitioners for the same land, I have determined to withdraw said petition and to represent anew, that the stock that I possed [possessed] at that time, and besides what I have since acquired, such as cattle and horses, have suffered much, for the want of a suitable place on which to keep them in a proper manner. Wherefore, I pray, Your Honor, to be pleased to grant me the place named Nipomo."[170]

The Nipomo land for which Dana was applying was sizeable. The somewhat vague boundaries he specified in his application – "the *Cañada* [open valley] of Suey on the South East; the *Avinal* [sandbed; actually spelled "*arenal*"] of the *arroyo* [a deep, stream-cut gully] of Santa Maria on the South West; the *arroyo* and *Cañada* of Temetate on the North West; and the *Lomas Montes* [low hills], the boundaries of San Luis, on the North East"[171] – indicate that the *rancho* comprised 10 to 11 square leagues of land, which equals 57,600 to 63,360 square acres. The 9½- by 12-inch *diseño* [map] submitted by Dana along with his application featured a crude sketch of the land. One can see Dana's rendition of the Temetate Range of mountains, the wide mesa upon which Nipomo rests, many small foothills, some creeks, and the dunes adjacent to the Pacific Ocean.[172] In the written application, Dana also had included a description of the land: "It is surrounded by hills, some of which are naked, and other covered with chamiso [an evergreen shrub often known as brushwood], as shown by the map herewith presented."[173]

The application set forth an extensive process of examination during which Dana was found to be in compliance with the Mexican legal requirements for receiving a land grant and his application forwarded to the Mexican Committee on Vacant Lands. Writing from Santa Barbara on December 10, 1835, two members of the committee endorsed Dana's application. In the words of Manuel Cota and Antonio Rodriguez, "The Committee on vacant lands, having examined the *Expediente* [file] instituted by Don Guillermo G. Dana, petitioning for the place of Nipomo, find that the land therein mentioned is vacant; that it pertains to the Pueblo of Los Berros (alias) La Purisima; that it is more than two leagues distant from said Pueblo; that is not needed by the same, since said *Pueblo* has more unoccupied land; ... that it is irrigable; that Don Guillermo G. Dana possesses such requisites, as under the law, entitle him to be heard on his petition. Wherefore, the Committee submits, for the deliberations of the *Ayuntamiento* [magistrate], the following proposition. 'The land named Nipomo, may be granted to Don Guillermo G. Dana.'"[174] The *ayuntamiento* of Santa Barbara, Francisco de la Guerra, wrote Governor Juan Bautista Alvarado four days later to give his approval of the committee's recommendation.[175] Dana's wait continued, though. It took until June 28, 1836, for Joaquin Carrillo, the administrator of Mission La Purisima, to confirm for the governor that "the said tract can be granted to [Dana], since this ex-mission does not need the same."[176]

Dana finally was granted the Nipomo land on April 6, 1837, when Governor Juan Bautista Alvarado was in Santa Barbara. The governor's proclamation began as follows: "In view of the petition, with which these proceedings commence, the report of the illustrious *Ayuntamiento* of Santa Barbara, with all other matters necessary to be considered, in conformity with the laws and regulations upon the subject, Don Guillermo Dana, is declared owner in property of the land known by the name of Nipomo."[177] It was the custom in those days for a land grant recipient to hold a ceremony upon taking actual possession of his land. Before representatives of the Mexican government, Dana performed the ceremony on May 25, 1837.

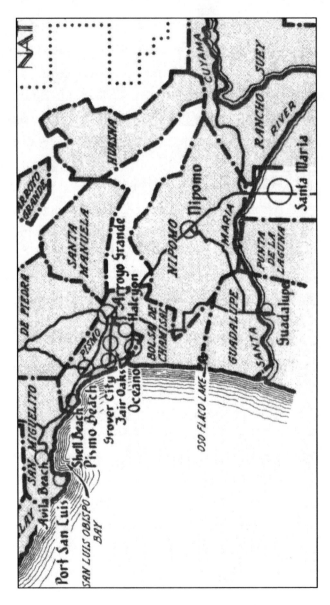

South San Luis Obispo County Land Grants

On May 10, 1842, Dana wrote a letter to the Justice of the Peace of Santa Barbara seeking official possession of his land. "I, Guillermo G. Dana, a Mexican citizen, and a resident of this Jurisdiction, before Your Honor, in due form of law, present myself and say; That having obtained a grant for the tract of land, known by the name of Nipomo, I apply to Your Honor, to the end, that you may be pleased to give me juridical possession of the same … Wherefore I pray, Your Honor, to be pleased to give me the possession asked, in which I will receive favor and justice; being pleased to admit this on common paper, there being none in this place of the corresponding seal."[178] Dana's request resulted in a juridical possession and survey of his land overseen by Joaquin Carrillo, now prefect of the District of Santa Barbara, on June 8, 1842. The evening of the survey, reported Carrillo in a memo written later, Dana, "accompanied by the Judge and witnesses [John Wilson and Antonio Rodriguez], intending as he said, to take the true, corporeal, and real possession of the said place of Nipomo … went upon said land, broke branches of trees, and scattered handsfull [sic] of earth, and made other demonstrations of the possession, which he said he took of said land, and I, the said Judge, ordered that from that time forward, Don Guillermo Dana should be considered the true owner and possessor of said lands."[179]

* * *

According to Dana family historian Alonzo Dana, Dana occupied his Nipomo rancho before receiving title to it. In 1835 or 1836, "Captain Dana moved stock upon the land and built a lean-to near the foothills southeast of where his ... adobe house now stands. A strong wind blew the first structure down and an adobe was built in the flat below where the present house stands. Later the creek overflowed during a wet winter and melted this adobe, which was set right on the ground. The last house ... is set on a rock foundation."[180] This final house, built on a foothill with a good view in all directions, was designed by Dana and constructed by Chumash employees under Dana's direction.[181] Construction materials included adobe gathered from soil nearby, lumber from the "San Rafael Mountains beyond Santa Ines Mission," and brea or tar from the Suey Rancho located along the Santa Maria River just south of Nipomo.[182] Originally featuring four rooms in one story, the house was expanded during Dana's lifetime to two stories and 14 rooms.

One of Dana's sons, Frank, recalled the details of the settlement of Rancho Nipomo. "In the fall of 1839 the [family] residence was permanently removed from Santa Barbara to Nipomo and Capt. Dana, being so far removed from all bases of supplies, early on saw that he must depend upon his own resources, and commenced to make preparations accordingly. Additions were made to the house for workshops, and the Indians, the only labor available at the time, were trained in some of the trades. ... By 1848 the house had grown large enough to contain ... one large room fitted with bins for the different grains

View of Dana Adobe from the southeast

View of Dana Adobe's courtyard

needed in the food supply, one milk room where butter and cheese were made, one room for a loom and spinning wheels, one for a blacksmith shop and one for a carpenter shop … one general storeroom and a kitchen."[183]

Known as Casa de Dana or the Dana Adobe, Dana's house now is regarded as an example of Yankee influence in Mexican California. While its adobe brick exterior typified Mexican-era buildings, its floor plan – with two rooms opening off either side of a central passageway, an interior fireplace, and windows – was reminiscent of the predominant New England architecture of the time. This fusion of California and New England influences became known as the Monterey Colonial architectural style. Writes architectural historian Harold Kirker: "Far from representing the pastoral life of the rancho, the Monterey Colonial house marks the first important victory in the inevitable struggle between the mutually antagonistic Spanish-Mexican and American cultures."[184] Kirker writes about how the prototype for this style, Thomas O. Larkin's home in Monterey, was popularized by word of mouth within the network of American settlers in California.[185]

* * *

Rancho Nipomo in Dana's time was a place of ruggedness and solitude. Juan Francisco, dictating his memoirs in the 1930s, described the scene: "A century ago, California was almost like Baja California remains today with a few scattered towns and military garrisons and vast stretches of land in between. Far apart were

Cave Landing

the large ranchos, miles from one another and lonesome perhaps, except that life was busy from daylight to dusk."[186] Continued Dana's son, "In those faroff days of the '30's and '40's, homes were few and far between. Cities were unknown and the few pueblos [towns] were also many leagues away … Each ranch, then, was a kingdom of its own."[187]

Despite the solitude, Dana maintained several bustling businesses on the Nipomo rancho. Among them were cattle, a thriving hide and tallow trade, sheep, soap, and other merchandise. Dana owned cattle, mostly for his family's own consumption and for hides and tallow. "It seems strange that few cows were milked in the old days," Juan Francisco writes. "They roamed practically wild over the Nipomo and when it was necessary to milk one, she had to be tied first … Cattle ran loose over the range, the only regulation being that a *ranchero* should not have above 1,000 head for each league of land in his possession."[188]   In the hide and tallow trade of the time, thousands of head of cattle were slaughtered at certain times of the year in what were called *matanzas*. The fat was boiled in large kettles and the resulting tallow packed for use in soap and candles. Hides were soaked in sea water and shipped to ports in foreign countries or to New England to be made into clothing, shoes, or boots.

Hide and tallow from the cattle would be traded for consumer goods at a warehouse owned by Dana at Cave Landing, an "excellent natural pier" located a mile south of the present town of Avila Beach.[189]   Juan Francisco said that as a youngster he often would help "take a carreta-load of hides and tallow if a ship was expected. Our 'leather dollars' … would be exchanged for commodities that we could not produce on Nipomo such as coffee, sugar, chocolate and clothing or furniture from the United States for our womenfolk."[190]   Frank Dana remembered, "The shipping was done from the landing in the bay of San Luis where ships would call for produce four or five times in a year. The ships came from Boston and were loaded with clothing, sweetmeats, and other luxuries, and a great deal of trading was done while they stopped in port."[191]   Other Dana family members recall that "at the Dana adobe there was a *cuarto de cueros* (hide room) … The hides were stacked high in there until taken to Cave Landing to use in exchange for goods brought in the coastal ships or those of the China trade: silks, satins, jade, ivory, tortoise shell combs…"[192] An 1846 shipment from Hawaii from Dana's cousin William Heath Davis Jr., included "calico prints, axes, and cherry cordial."[193]

Sheep, soap, and other merchandise also had places in the business of Dana's rancho. According to Juan Francisco, sheep were raised at Nipomo, and "blankets, serapes and other products were woven from the wool on our rancho."[194] Dana also produced soap: "When the soap was made it was very much like Castile soap and was very good and solid," the younger Dana wrote later. "My father exchanged it for hides and other produce among his friends."[195] With the raw materials acquired from ships passing by Cave Landing, Dana engaged in handy work.

Dana's living room was called the sala

Juan Francisco writes of "stores of furniture, clothing, and implements made in our blacksmith shop."[196] The captain even owned a still, "where he made a little whiskey for trade purposes."[197]

Writes historian Ferol Egan of the lifestyle of Yankee landowners such as Dana: "It was a gentle culture, with a charm and a kind of innocence. ... The *Californios* enjoyed a life of ease and pleasure. *Majordomos* and *vaqueros* did the hard work, and the ranchero concentrated upon a lifestyle that refused to be hurried. He gave and attended a multitude of fiestas. He participated in annual rodeos or roundups. He watched amateur bullfights or bear-and-bull fights, bet on cock fights and horse races; roped grizzly bears for sport; and saw to it that all family weddings, christenings, and funerals were carried out in the grand style befitting a *Californio*. It was a time of gracious living in a good land, a time of pastoral grace."[198]

* * *

As his family was growing, as he moved his family from Santa Barbara to Nipomo, and as he focused on the many business opportunities of the day, Dana also was undergoing what appears to be a deep, heartfelt conversion to Catholicism. Prior to his baptism in San Diego, Dana had been a churchgoer; Stephen Reynolds' Hawaii journal recounts at least one instance of Dana attending "meeting" along with other Yankees on Sundays.[199] Dana thus must have had some understanding of the significance of leaving the Puritan-inspired faith of his native Massachusetts in favor of a distinctly different type of Christianity.

Dana, accordingly, appears to have taken his Catholicism quite seriously. In 1838, for instance, he baptized into the Catholic faith a man who had been mortally wounded at Rancho Nipomo. The story of the murder comes from Faxon Dean Atherton, who later wrote a journal of his California travels in 1836-1839. On March 3, 1838, Atherton traveled by horse from San Luis Obispo to Nipomo with Thomas Stuart, an employee of Dana's who during the trip became "drunk" after taking several drinks from Atherton's bottle of brandy.[200] Continues Atherton: "About 5 p.m. we arrived at Nipomo. Found Capt. Dana there, with whom Stuart immediately commenced a dispute on account of a black that Capt. D had brought to the house with him, against whom it appears that Stuart had some grudge. A few moments afterwards he commenced with the black (whose name was 'Bill') behind the house … I went in and commenced reading and in a short time the black came to the door holding his hand before his breast from which the blood was flowing in a stream of an inch in thickness at least. I immediately saw that he had been stabbed and was seeking assistance. As the poor fellow was so far gone, he could not speak. I jumped up to get out doors and as I passed him the blood spurted all over me. He instantly turned round, headed towards me and fell on the ground struggling for breath. Capt. D, at the same time coming round the corner of the house and seeing at a

HISTORY OF THE ⅌ BRAND

THE BRAND OF WILLIAM G. DANA WAS RECORDED IN "INGRESOS AL FONDO MUNICIPAL" IN SANTA BARBARA, JUNE 16, 1836.

AFTER STATEHOOD, BRAND REGISTRY WAS DONE BY THE COUNTY RECORDER. THE FOLLOWING PARAGRAPH WAS TAKEN FROM THE SAN LUIS OBISPO COUNTY BOOK OF RECORDS.

"THE WITHIN MARK WAS PRESENTED THIS 4th DAY OF NOV. A.D. 1857 BY WM. G. DANA & IS KNOWN AS THE BRAND OF HIS HORSES & CATTLE".

THE BRAND OF WM. G. DANA IS THE FIFTH BRAND RECORDED IN SAN LUIS OBISPO COUNTY IN THE BOOK OF BRANDS.

IN 1919, THE STATE OF CALIFORNIA ASSUMED RESPONSIBILITY FOR THE BRAND REGISTRY AND ⨊ WAS REGISTERED TO GEORGE O. DANA, NIPOMO, CALIF.

IN 1946 THE BRAND WAS TRANSFERRED TO GEORGE O. DANA, GEORGE J. DANA, AND ANDREW RENETZKY dba GEORGE O. DANA & SON CATTLE CO. NIPOMO.

ON OCTOBER 26, 1989 THE BRAND WAS TRANSFERRED TO GEORGE O. AND JAMES T. DANA, NIPOMO CALIF.

glance the state the poor fellow was in, baptized him calling myself and an Indian who was present to witness it. After he laid about 15 minutes, finding he was still struggling for life, [we] took [him] inside the house. Capt. D asked him how he felt and answering in Spanish said, '*Muy malo,*' which was all he said that could be understood. About 12 midnight he died ... Stuart came round to the front of the house about the time the Negro fell, having a knife in his hand bloody to the hilt, stating at the same time that he had told him if he returned again to the Rancho he would kill [him] and that he had kept his word. This he repeated a number of times, but he appeared to be perfectly mad at the time."[201]   According to Atherton, Stuart regained rationality and at Dana's behest turned himself in, ending up in the jail at Mission La Purisima.[202]   Bill, too, wound up at La Purisima, in the mission's cemetery. His burial notice, dated March 16, 1838, describes "Guillermo, surname unknown, birthplace unknown, an adult who died on Rancho Nipomo, having been baptized at the point of death by Don Guillermo Dana."[203]

Dana's own cattle brand, registered in Santa Barbara in June 1836, bore a connection to his Catholic faith. According to family lore, Dana identified his livestock with a brand that was a modification of the "Chi-Rho," a Christian symbol that would have been displayed on the altars of missions and chapels Dana attended. In the "Chi-Rho," the Greek letters "P" and "X" – the first two letters of the word "Christ" in Greek – are superimposed onto each other. Dana took the "P" from the "Chi-Rho" and added a wavy line underneath, reportedly to represent his many years as an ocean trader. The brand is still being used nearly two centuries later by Dana descendants.

Finally, Catholicism was part of the daily life of Dana and his wife, Maria Josefa. His son, Juan Francisco, wrote of his family's morning custom "to open all the windows and sing the morning hymn to the Virgin upon arising. This was led by our Spanish mother."[204]   Dana and his wife would host priests at their home. Juan Francisco remembered that, on these occasions, Maria Josefa "converted the parlor

**Adelina's burial marker,
Mission San Luis Obispo**

The inscription reads:

**"This lovely bud so young and fair
Called hence by early doom;
Just came to show how sweet a flower
In Paradise could bloom."**

into a temporary chapel which was the custom if a rancho did not have its own chapel."[205]   Dana's acquaintance with a particular priest, Father Jose Miguel Gomez of Mission San Luis Obispo, resulted in the granting of a special favor. When the Danas' five-year-old daughter Adelina Eliza died in April 1847, Father Gomez allowed her to be buried within the mission walls. Today, visitors to Mission San Luis Obispo can see her burial marker in the rear west wall of the church.

* * *

As Dana was building his life in California, he was receiving validation of his decision to settle there. His old business associate, Stephen Reynolds, wrote Dana on March 17, 1836, to describe the situation in Oahu: "We are almost overrun with the missionaries, seamen's preachers, and train of native hypocrites. ... The times are bad here; little doing; money all gone to Canton; what we are to do is hard to tell. ... We do not get enough to eat now."[206]   Reynolds gave his friend counsel. "Send us a good lot of hides. Stick to your farm, so when hunger drives me hence I may find you with a spare loaf for a poor old friend. I am truly glad your prospects are good for becoming a wealthy farmer. Stick to it! Stick, stick, stick, stick, stick to it. Go slow, go sure; you have nothing to fear."[207]

NIPOMO: SIDING WITH FREMONT
AND THE UNITED STATES

Dana, who had adjusted quite well to the governance and culture of Mexican California, became unwillingly involved in power struggles between the Mexican governors and revolutionary native Californians from the north. The continuing internecine squabbles took a toll on Dana, and he ultimately decided to openly side with Americans seeking to occupy California.

The intrigues began in 1837, when Dana supported his father-in-law, Don Carlos Carrillo, for the office of governor. Carrillo, who was legally appointed as provisional governor by the president of Mexico, faced the opposition of revolutionaries from the north led by Juan Bautista Alvarado and Jose Castro. An October 1836 letter from then-governor Nicolas Gutierrez addresses Dana *"mi estimado amigo"* [my esteemed friend], indicating the probability of Dana's support for the loyalist party represented by Gutierrez.[208] Unfortunately for Dana, he picked the wrong side: Alvarado ultimately won the battle for the governorship with Carrillo, Gutierrez, and others, taking Carrillo prisoner (and releasing him shortly thereafter) in late 1838.

In mid-1838, Dana reportedly helped his father-in-law elude forces commanded by Alvarado. In Los Angeles on May 20, Alvarado's forces arrested Carrillo, Carrillo's brother, and some of their supporters. Some of the detainees were taken to Sonoma, while Don Carlos was allowed to remain in Santa Barbara. Don Carlos escaped, fleeing "to the beach by himself to look for the boat that his son-in-law, Don Guillermo Dana, had sent from Santa Barbara, just in case it might be needed. He managed to find it and set sail in the direction of the Baja California frontier. … That is how Don Carlos Carrillo ended his tenure in government."[209]

Having appointed himself governor of the state, Alvarado must have kept his grudge against Dana. In 1840, Alvarado acted on rumors of a forthcoming Texas-style coup and mounted a campaign against American-born residents not naturalized as Mexican citizens. The armed forces of Alvarado arrested John Michael Price, then in the service of Dana as a *vaquero* at Dana's ranch. As Juan Francisco Dana, a witness to the event, recounted: "No one was more surprised than my father when a band of soldiers appeared at Casa de Dana one morning with a warrant for Price's arrest. *Tio Juan* was taken to Santa Barbara where he joined the rest of the prisoners in a damp, unventilated room at the mission."[210] It has been said that arresting Price while leaving Dana undisturbed was as far as Alvarado "thought prudent to go against so powerful a man in resenting his adherence to the opposite party."[211] Price was released soon thereafter; later, Price became a prominent landowner in the Pismo Beach area. Dana did shelter other Americans at his rancho. Dana's cousin, William Heath Davis Jr., writes of stopping in Nipomo in 1840 and finding two young Americans, Henry F. Teschemacher and Dr. Nicholas A. Den, under Dana's protection.[212] Teschemacher went on to be mayor of San Francisco, and in 1842 Den was awarded a Mexican land grant in the Santa Barbara area.

Alvarado stepped down in 1842, and Manuel Micheltorena assumed the governorship, but that did not mean Dana's troubles were over. In 1844, Alvarado, Castro, and Pio Pico conspired against Micheltorena in another revolution. As William Heath Davis Jr., Dana's cousin, wrote later, the kindling for the insurgency was a combination of the rebel leaders' ambition and a popular distaste for the *cholo* soldiers brought into California from Mexico by Micheltorena. "General Castro ... was ambitious, and naturally joined with Alvarado," Davis wrote. "There was also a good deal of feeling by many against the troops who came into the country with Micheltorena, especially by the residents of Monterey, where the troops were quartered, they alleging that the soldiers stole their chickens and committed other small depredations. They might have done something worse, though there is no evidence of it."[213]

According to Davis, wealthy *rancheros* such as Dana opposed the revolution. "They desired peace, naturally, as they had everything to lose by conflict and nothing to gain," he wrote.[214] Still, the conflict continued. After a skirmish with Micheltorena and his force in the Salinas area, Alvarado and Castro retreated, and marched their troops south for the purpose of "visiting the different ranchos, creating sympathy for their cause and obtaining recruits, horses and provisions. Alvarado ... induced some of the rancheros to join him. Many of the younger men were taken against their will as recruits for his army. He also secured a large number of horses, some of which were given to him voluntarily and others taken by force."[215]

During this drive south by Alvarado and Castro, Dana himself was briefly detained by a rebel regiment commanded by Joaquin Valenzuela, a militant revolutionary charged with the task of flushing out and arresting supporters of Micheltorena. William A. Streeter, an American prisoner who accompanied Valenzuela on the march, described, but did not date, the event: "The next morning we marched into Nipomo. Arrived here, Valenzuela arrested Dana, telling him that he must go with him to Los Angeles."[216] Dana, however, was rescued by Manuel Castro, a superior of Valenzuela's who "had heard of Valenzuela's threat to kill all the Americans he found and had hurried forward to prevent him from carrying it into execution."[217] Streeter wrote about Dana's release: "Dana appealed to Castro declaring that it was impossible to leave his family alone and unprotected and if he must of necessity go, I would have to be left to take care of his family. Castro turned to Valenzuela and ordered him to release Capt. Dana, and also [Francis Ziba] Branch, who said that his family too had been left wholly unprotected. Accordingly, Dana remained at Nipomo and Branch returned to San Luis Obispo."[218]

Branch later became the owner of a large parcel in the Arroyo Grande Valley.

Micheltorena ultimately capitulated on February 22, 1845, with the Treaty of Cahuenga. Pio Pico became governor, and Jose Castro became *comandante general*. Dana, however, could not have been very favorable toward the new government. Reeling from the harassment he had taken for nearly a decade from Alvarado and others, he had to have been hoping anew for a Yankee takeover of California.

* * *

Dana's hospitality in 1846 for a battalion of soldiers commanded by Lieutenant Colonel John Charles Fremont documented Dana's readiness to actively support the United States. Fremont, under orders from Commodore Robert F. Stockton, was heading south to capture Santa Barbara during the Mexican-American War. On December 17, Fremont's troops concluded a 15-mile march from San Luis Obispo by setting up camp near Dana's ranch, in a "wide, valley-like *arroyo*" through which the Los Berros Creek runs.[219] Fremont apparently knew he was in favorable surroundings: The country surrounding Nipomo reportedly "was not known to contain any Californian party."[220] There is some disagreement on the size of Fremont's battalion. One article lists its size as "about a hundred,"[221] while another source describes it as including "375 whites … and fifty Walla Walla Indians."[222] Fremont's battalion reportedly was "equipped with a cannon, a wagon train, and a great number of pack mules."[223]

Fremont's route to Santa Barbara

Lt. Col. John C. Fremont

Dana was friendly to Fremont and his men. He rode out to the camp to invite Fremont to dine with him, ordered beef for the soldiers, and sold bread to some of them. Juan Francisco, who was eight at the time of the visit, told the story: "It was during the month of December that my father heard that the colonel and his men had left San Luis Obispo and were camped about three miles northeast of our casa, in an oak grove. My father prepared to go over to the camp and greet them. It was rainy weather and Fremont's company surely looked cold and weary."[224] Dana reportedly ordered 40 head of beef for Fremont's men. "Fremont and six of his officers," Juan Francisco continued, "were invited to the casa for lunch with us and I was allowed the great privilege of sitting at the table right next to the great soldier. … Fremont made friends with everyone at our place."[225]

Edwin Bryant, a member of Fremont's battalion, described his stay at Dana's. "We encamped about three o'clock near the rancho of Captain Dana," he said, "in a large and handsome valley well watered by an *arroyo*. Captain Dana is a native of Massachusetts, and has resided in this country about thirty years. He is known and esteemed throughout California for his intelligence and private virtues, and his unbounded generosity and hospitality. I purchased here a few loaves of wheat bread, and distributed them among the men belonging to our company as far as they would go, a luxury which they have not indulged in since the commencement of the march."[226]

Dana gave Fremont both supplies and counsel on how to avoid a force of native Californians awaiting the Americans at Gaviota Pass. He referred Fremont to William Foxen, a friend and fellow *ranchero* who knew more about the territory surrounding Gaviota. According to Juan Francisco, Fremont and Dana "had a private talk after the meal and we were later told that he had told my father about the scarcity of supplies for his men and wondered if my father could help."[227] Dana offered Fremont "a supply of fresh beef and thirty horses" and "Fremont wrote an order on the United States government for payment" but Dana replied that he would never present it for payment.[228] As regards Dana's advice to Fremont, he "may have told Fremont to question Foxen about proceeding to Santa Barbara."[229] Dana apparently "well knew the sentiment of the *paisanos* toward the Americans who were invading their country and advised Fremont to camp next at the rancho of Tinaquaic, belonging to ... Foxen. This was located southeast of our lands toward Santa Barbara where Fremont was heading ... Whether Father had heard that Agustin Janssen was gathering a force of Californios to resist the invaders, or whether he only suspected that something was afoot, I do not know."[230] According to Bryant's diary, the battalion left Nipomo on the morning of December 19. Camp was made 18 miles from Dana's, near the head of the Santa Maria Valley.

Foxen ultimately helped Fremont elude Janssen and the Californians situated at the Gaviota Pass, where "an ambush had been prepared ... and huge boulders were being loosened to be pushed down by the Californios on the gringos as they went through."[231] Foxen guided Fremont and his troops south by way of the mountainous San Marcos Pass. Foxen, as related by Juan Francisco, shared Dana's desire for a Yankee takeover. "Like my father and other farseeing men of that period, he saw a change in rule for California was needed but it was a touchy subject at the time."[232] Fremont and his regiment marched unscathed into Santa Barbara.

Fremont's battalion returned to Dana's on February 4, 1847. "About noon on the 4th," wrote Bryant in his diary, "we halted at the rancho of Captain Dana, where we procured fresh horses, leaving our wretchedly lean and tired animals, and proceeding on, stopped for the night at the rancho of Mr. [Francis Ziba] Branch."[233]   Despite the help they had given Fremont and his men, neither Dana nor Foxen was mentioned directly in Fremont's memoir about his time in California. Two members of Dana's family, however, did not escape the eye of Lieutenant Louis McLane, a naval artillery officer who commanded an ammunition wagon in Fremont's battalion. McLane observed that Dana had "married a Californian woman who, though the mother of 11 children, is still handsome. [Dana] has a fine property and a really beautiful daughter [Maria Josefa, then 17 years old]."[234]

* * *

According to a story handed down by Dana's son Juan Francisco and others, Fremont's men may not have repaid the kindness shown them by Dana. The story revolves around Dana's provision of horses to Fremont. "When my father had given the order for the thirty horses to be rounded up, he also gave orders about certain horses which were not to be taken," wrote Juan Francisco.[235] Fremont's soldiers, however, defied Dana's instructions by taking Dana's personal horse and the personal mounts of Maria Josefa and one of the daughters, leaving only an old *caponera*, or "bell-mare," behind.[236]

As the story goes, this proved to be the soldiers' mistake. When a new horse was purchased, it was common practice among *rancheros* to tie the new steed to an older bell-mare with a short rope. The two horses "would run over the fields for a few days until they became acquainted. This process would be repeated with other horses until a *caballada* was formed … Whatever happened, a horse would never desert his own *caballada* no matter with how many others he might roam over pasture and *loma*."[237]

This was a detail overlooked by Fremont's soldiers. To continue Juan Francisco's story, Dana sent some of his vaqueros to Fremont's encampment in Foxen Canyon. "The vaqueros crept upon the men guarding the horses and set the bell-mare loose. The vaqueros then stampeded the horses and in the wild confusion that immediately followed all the horses were scattered and our *caponera* was reunited with the missing horses."[238] The missing horses were back in Nipomo "in a day or so."[239]

* * *

After assisting Fremont, Dana helped a Yankee regiment commanded by Colonel Jonathan Drake Stevenson of New York. The "Stevenson Regiment" was given by President James Polk the task of facilitating, in the wake of an anticipated American victory in the Mexican War, the colonization of California. The regiment arrived in California in March and April of 1847.

John McHenry Hollingsworth, a lieutenant under Stevenson's command, wrote in his journal of an 1848 visit by the regiment to Dana's ranch. "As we were getting to our journeys [sic] end, I made a stop of four days to recruit,

Col. Jonathan Stevenson

my worn out animals, at the ranch of Capt Damers [Dana]. I did not at first pitch my tents, near the house, but upon his hearing that I was encamped near, he sent for me to come and take supper with him. The next day I moved my encampment close to the house. He was very kind to me made me take all my meals at his house. His pretty daughter [Maria Josefa] always sat at the head of the table and appeared to be a kind hearted girl. I took leave of this place with some regret and moved on as rapidly as possible."[240]

In a February 7, 1849, letter written to Dr. John S. Griffin, Stevenson himself told of his leaving of animals in Nipomo. "At Captain Dana's on my way up I left my Pico horse and the large Bay ... and Bonny left the little black that Carrillo gave me and a yellow horse belonging to

Colgan, one of my men, together with his saddle & bridle.
… Bonny left four mules and Holly one jenny mule at the
Captains [sic] – in all ten animals they will be worth if no
others are recovered $2500 in San Francisco or Pueblo San
Jose."[241]

Stevenson, who had lost 51 animals out of a
caballada of 64 between Los Angeles and Monterey on an
unsuccessful trip to the mines, hoped to recover as many
as possible. In the letter he ordered Griffin to take back
animals left at Dana's ranch and at other ranches: "I enclose
you a full authority in both English and Spanish to take and
recover all animals & property belonging to me which you
find on your way up."[242]

One historian of the period believed Dana might
have contemplated military service to the United States
were he not "feeling ill" at the time.[243] Nevertheless,
through assistance to the units of Fremont and Stevenson,
Dana found a way to help bring about the result he had
been talking and thinking about for a long time: a Yankee
conquest of California.

* * *

Perhaps hoping to gain the favor of the territory's
new rulers, Dana served the United States government by
allowing his house to be a meeting place in the first postal
service in California. In April 1847, California's military
governor, General Stephen W. Kearny, established mail
service between San Francisco and San Diego. General
William Tecumseh Sherman, in an 1889 article recalling

his time as an Army lieutenant in California, described the arrangement: "Captain [Joseph] Folsom divided the mail route into four parts – San Francisco to Monterey, Monterey to 'Dana's' (Nepoma), Dana's to Los Angeles, and Los Angeles to San Diego. … The mail-rider from Monterey to Dana's was an old trapper, Jim Beckwourth … a cross between a voyageur of Canada and a Crow Indian."[244] The service began on April 1, with Juan Francisco "still young enough to be thrilled when I saw the couriers stop at our Casa to change their mail pouches and horses and continue on their way north or south along the old Camino Real."[245] The Dana home did not last for long as a mail stop, however. "Sometime in the middle '50's a regular post office came to the new county seat [San Luis Obispo] and the days of reading our neighbor's newspapers were over," he wrote later. "The Casa de Dana also stopped being a post stop then as mail arrived at San Luis Obispo by both boat or stage."[246]

Word of Dana's support for the Yankees spread eastward. Dana's sister Adeline, now married and living in New York, wrote her brother in January, 1849: "I am constrained, dear William, despite my mortification, to say that I have not received a letter from you in 18 years!"[247] She continued, "I have written you several times of late – the last communication forwarded by Alfred Robinson of this City [New York] who had gone to reside in San Francisco, and who, I have been informed, married a cousin of your wife's … As I have, my dear brother, not heard from you in eighteen years."[248]   Finally, she told her brother he had received publicity in the East. "I have seen your name repeatedly in some journals of travelers through California," she wrote. "Colonel Fremont in his tour speaks of you as 'The friendly Captain Dana' who tendered him hospitality. G.W. Bryant [Edwin Bryant] … describes you … as a 'gentleman whose unbounded liberality and hospitality is known throughout California'."[249]

NIPOMO:
AN AMERICAN ONCE AGAIN

The conquest completed, Dana's desire for American rule over California was fulfilled. Dana now was determined to capitalize on the opportunity and remain involved in California affairs. Dana welcomed Yankees new to California in 1848, when the United States steamship Edith was grounded off the central California coast. Historical accounts differ; according to Juan Francisco, the ship was deliberately grounded by her crew. "Right down near Point Arguello, the U.S.S. Edith was abandoned by her crew. They must have thought they were nearer to the gold fields than they actually were. ... The story, as we learned it, was that ... as the ship Edith neared the Point the sailors deliberately ran her onto a sandbar and grounded her."[250]

After vacating their vessel, the sailors soon ran into Dana's ranch. "As our Casa de Dana was the only stopping place," Juan Francisco continued, "the crew as well as the passengers eventually knocked on our door. Some of the people stayed on for several days but the sailors could hardly wait to start off to the mines. My father even gave the deserters money and horses to start them on their way north."[251] The daughter of Maria Josefa Pollard, Dana's oldest daughter, has said that during the stay of the Edith's sailors at the rancho "a beef each day and many sheep were slaughtered."[252]   According to Dana's granddaughter Virginia de la Cuesta, the crew stayed "about three weeks" before heading on to Monterey.[253]

As he had done in the building of the schooner <u>La Fama</u> two decades before, Dana made use of the remnants of a sunken ship. He sent a crew to salvage materials from the <u>Edith</u>; in fact, the vessel's smokestack reportedly was made into the forge in his blacksmith shop. Dana took "a large quantity of copper" and "a good quality of anthracite coal" from the <u>Edith</u>.[254]   In addition, he appears to have used some of the wood to build a structure on his ranch and sold some of the unneeded materials. George W. B. Evans, a forty-niner who had traveled to California from Ohio, happened by Dana's land on his way north. In his journal, he refers to a gentleman who presumably was Dana or one of Dana's employees: "Oct. 5. One and a half mile's travel this morning brought us to Ranch Nepomo [sic], where we found an American selling goods. One of our party sold him a mule, and here we found a part of the wreck of the propeller, of New York, which boat went ashore five weeks ago on this coast. ... This gentleman had brought in some of the irons of the boat and a portion of the main mast. He is now engaged in building a hewed log house, the first seen on our route since leaving Texas."[255]   Dana also extracted from the <u>Edith</u> a large round mahogany table that now is on display at the Dana Adobe.

* * *

During this period Dana benefited from the enormous economic prosperity associated with the California Gold Rush. As a wealthy *ranchero* with plenty of land for cattle and sheep, he and his family received some of their "highest living years" due to the Gold Rush stimulus.[256]

The wellspring of Dana's Gold Rush good fortune was the cattle business. With the discovery of gold, the price of cattle promptly soared from $2 and $4 a head to $20 and $50, and cattle ranchers such as Dana became wealthy.[257] His *rancho* reportedly received as much as $85 a head at the boom's height.[258] Before the gold mining days, Juan Francisco wrote, "Our cattle had been slaughtered in large numbers merely for their hides and tallow but during the '50's when the demand for meat was so high, forty to fifty dollars a head was a usual price."[259] He described the days when he and his father used to drive their cattle to San Mateo, where it would be sold for "very high prices and consigned to the gold mining country. ... The San Francisco buyers would come down and either take over delivery at that point or hire our *vaqueros* for the short drive to San Francisco."[260] Dana himself was quite pleased with the cattle economy, as attested by William H. Thomes, who encountered Dana at Cave Landing in the mid-1840s. "We picked up about a thousand hides here, and also had some company, among the latter Captain Dana, whom we had met several times before on our first visit. He said that he was very well contented with his life at San Luis, and had all the land and cattle that he desired, and when we asked him how many head, he laughed, and stated that he did not know the exact number, as he had not rounded in and branded for two years. He must have had confidence in his neighbors."[261]   Dana's son Frank, reminiscing about these days, wrote, "Cattle were allowed to run at large, and it was not imperative to keep them within bounds. ... The only regulation existing was that a person should not have above one thousand head for every league of land in his possession."[262]

Prices of California stock plummeted as soon as cattle herds began to be driven overland to the mines. The "good days for Nipomo," according to Juan Francisco," ... certainly didn't last forever because as the mining operations increased so did transportation and many other things could now be purchased. ... So by 1852 these very high prices became a thing of the past."[263]   Still, he remembered his father made money from the cattle business as late as 1858. In 1856, Dana reportedly purchased "500 yearling steers and 200 heifers" at the low price of "five to seven dollars a head."[264]   Two years later, Dana sold the cattle he had bought, along with some of his own stock, for $24,000.[265]

Dana also profited from the sheep trade. Elaborates Frank Dana, "Sheep were raised on the Nipomo rancho from my earliest recollection, and I believe they must have been brought to the rancho very early in the period between 1840 and 1845. These sheep were of the breed which were afterward called New Mexican after the discovery of gold in

California. ... It was from the wool of these sheep that the blankets and other fabrics were made. ... These sheep to the number of 2,000 were sold during the boom subsequent on the discovery of gold."[266]   Frank added that, "about 1852," his father purchased another band of sheep for use as meat. "These sheep were ... of a very coarse breed, but they were big and hardy. They were never shorn, and only when wool was needed for a mattress it was taken for that purpose."[267]

In all, the thriving stock business allowed Dana and his family to flourish. "During the gold rush and days for about fifteen years after, I think we *rancheros* had the most affluent times we have ever seen," said Juan Francisco. "We had lived a very simple life in California before 1849 and even the transition from Mexican to American rule had hardly affected life on the distant *ranchos*. After gold had been discovered, every bullock on our rolling hills seemed worth his weight in gold."[268]   The surge of prosperity even seemed to change the Dana family's lifestyle. "With this sudden wealth ... everyone found that he needed more clothes, more furniture, more *fiestas* – and more imported things from around the Horn. No longer were 'homemade' things good enough. Looking back, I suppose we were improvident but we thought the fabulous cattle prices would keep on forever."[269]   The December 26, 1853, last will and testament of Dana and his wife Maria Josefa lists their holdings as "said horned cattle being estimated at about the number of Two Thousand, said horses and mares at about One Hundred, and said sheep at about Four Hundred."[270]

Juan Francisco Dana

**Four of the Dana boys: from left,
Frank, David, Edward, Juan**

* * *

The creation of San Luis Obispo County, with Nipomo within its boundaries and Mission San Luis Obispo designated as the county seat, created more business opportunities for Dana. In 1850, Dana helped make one of the first wagon roads in the county, a road between San Luis Obispo and Santa Rosa Creek, near present-day Cambria. He used the road the same year to haul the timber used in building the county's first frame building, a large edifice he called "Casa Grande." The building, which reportedly cost Dana $50,000, was used as a hotel, saloon, business building, and courthouse. Built of adobe walls and pine lumber, and featuring an iron roof, Casa Grande, also known as "Dana House," was located downtown, near what is now the intersection of Court and Monterey streets in present-day San Luis Obispo.

The building's role as a hotel provides the context for a revealing anecdote about Dana. In 1915, at the age of 90, Frederick Wickenden, the son-in-law of William Foxen, reminisced for his son Ernest about an undated period when he ran the hotel for Dana. During this time, Frederick had difficulty with Native American servants in his employ. Writes Ernest: "One day, the Indian cook, with a knife, chased his dishwasher through the dining room. This led to a lot of fighting. Father managed to catch the Indians and tied their arms behind them. Then he sent word to William Dana to come up and punish the fellows.

When Dana, who was a kindly man, got there, he gave each a slight tap on the back with his cane, saying, 'Carrajos, don't do that again,' and ordered them released."[271]

Dana's rapport with Native Americans can be traced to his decades of exposure to different cultures and peoples. In Nipomo, he hired Chumash laborers to build his home and to do much of the work on his rancho. Juan Francisco stated, "From my earliest childhood I grew up along with the Indians on our rancho. Those who were employed both in the house or on the range were trusted by all of us and made good workmen."[272]   Juan Francisco writes of Chumash employees' work in a spinning shop, a saddle shop, and a blacksmith shop located on the rancho; he also describes their contributions to *matanzas*, the large-scale slaughter of cattle for their hides and tallow. Chumash lived in small homes "around the outskirts of the rancho"; for their efforts, Dana "paid the men $8.00 a month and board besides rationing to the families items like flour, beans, and meat."[273]   Dana and his wife were hospitable to Native Americans, according to Juan Francisco. "Indians from the surrounding country were friendly and in my youth they would gather around our casa when they came visiting and my mother always fed them and treated them as kindly as she did everyone."[274]

Juan Francisco defends the reputation of the Native Americans of his area. "Every now and then I read some newspaper account about hostile Indians in this part of California, and in fairness to the Indians that I knew, I want to say that there never were any hostile Indians here in my time. Such stories are all wrong. Most of our Indians were the so-called coastal Indians, Canaliños is the correct name for them. These Indians were a simple, good-natured, hard-working, faithful, and honest lot of people long before my time. They were all good Catholics, and there was never any trouble among them that couldn't be settled by a few words from any priest."[275] As remembered by Juan Francisco, the Chumash language of Canaliño was taught to the Dana children along with Spanish and English.[276]

Dana's affinity for the less privileged was observed by others. United States Consul Thomas Oliver Larkin, in a June 15, 1846, dispatch to Secretary of State James Buchanan, praised Dana's character in a description of "principal men" of California. Dana, listed under "Ex-Mission of San Luis," was portrayed by Larkin as follows: "William Dana, formerly Sea Captain, now Farmer. Born in Massechusetts [sic]. Aged about 50 years. Over twenty years a resident of California. Married in the Carrello [sic] family. A man of some wealth, of much respectability of character, of good and honest intentions, often Alcalde of Santa Barbara. Well versed in the general information of the day. Much looked up to by the poorer people, and of influence with them. Never connected with the political characters of the day."[277] Larkin knew Dana personally; in November 1846, just five months after writing this dispatch, Larkin visited Rancho Nipomo.[278]

* * *

Henry A. Tefft

Dana became indirectly involved in the writing of the state constitution through the involvement of his future son-in-law in California's first Constitutional Convention. Henry A. Tefft was a young lawyer from Wisconsin who settled in the San Luis Obispo area in 1849. Tefft became acquainted with Dana, and lived at Dana's home in Nipomo for a four-month stretch.[279] During this time, Tefft "practiced law and became known and respected in the area."[280] Due to his blossoming reputation and Dana's support, Tefft was elected as San Luis Obispo County's delegate to the state's Constitutional Convention in Monterey. One of the first 10 delegates to be seated at Colton Hall in August 1849, Tefft was appointed secretary pro tempore of the

Maria Josefa Dana Tefft Pollard

convention and served on committees that determined how the constitution would be written and how many delegates from each area would be seated. Tefft was a vocal participant in the convention, arguing in favor of the right of Native Americans to vote, property rights for women, the establishment of county schools, and a "Homestead Exemption" clause enabling a homeowner to have his home declared exempt from seizure for the payment of debts. The new Constitution of California was completed on October 12, 1849, and Tefft rode south, taking the responsibility of "distributing copies to the southern part of the state."[281]

There is no way to know the degree to which Tefft's positions at the convention were influenced, if at all, by his mentor Dana. Nevertheless, it is logical to assume that Tefft was closely aligned with his future father-in-law. Upon his return from the convention, Tefft was elected as San Luis Obispo County's first assemblyman and during his term played a key role in the passage of a law implementing the Homestead Exemption clause. Later, when the state legislature divided the state into judicial districts, Tefft was elected as the first district judge of the Second Judicial District (comprised of San Luis Obispo and Santa Barbara counties). In July 1850, Tefft married Dana's oldest daughter, Maria Josefa, in a wedding ceremony conducted at Rancho Nipomo. Tefft was either 25 or 26 at the time; Maria Josefa was 20 or 21.

Tefft's best man at the wedding was William Rich Hutton, who was 24 when he visited Nipomo for the nuptials. By this time, Hutton already had accepted an appointment as county surveyor of San Luis Obispo County. Hutton, also a paymaster for the U.S. volunteer forces, included a detailed description of the wedding in a recollection written years later. The wedding was a grand affair, with many attendees. "Days before the wedding day the relations began to arrive – Hosts of beautiful & graceful girls & hosts of handsome matrons also – (crowds) of men both young and old, all cousins of the bride's mother '*mi prima Chefista*' … On the day before the wedding the *parientes* [relatives] of the bride began to come early in the day. Relationships in California were counted as in Virginia, consequently the house was somefilled up. … The actual wedding could not be seen. It was the usual ceremony of the Catholic Church. The day was passed by the men in chiefly feats of horsemanship – and later in the dance – Numbers of people other than relations had come from the country around and the place was all confusion."[282]   In another letter to his mother, Hutton shared his assessment of Dana: "I found Captain Dana an excellent good-natured old gentleman. ... Since I have been here they have treated me very kindly, and they live very comfortably."[283]

Hutton's observations about Dana's daughter Maria Josefa reveal a bit about the education of Dana's children. "With Mrs. Tefft ... that in which she most differs from her 'paisana' is in her love for reading. Altho' she has had but few books she knows them by heart – among others, Moratin's Comedies and 'Poesias Sueltas'."[284]   Alonzo Dana recalls that Dana hired a music teacher from San Francisco to give his daughters monthly lessons in "music and piano."[285] The Danas made education a higher priority for the boys. Juan Francisco Dana writes of his and his brothers' attendance at a school for boys at Mission Santa Ines. "Parents paid $150 for every boy entered per year," he wrote.[286]   Juan Francisco and some of his brothers also attended the Benicia Collegiate Institute in Benicia. Brothers Charles and Henry reportedly attended college in the East, staying with their father's sister, Adeline Darling.[287] As further evidence of Dana's commitment to education, Dana sponsored the education of his brother-in-law. Leo Carrillo, grandson of Pedro Carrillo, writes that Dana paid for Pedro, younger than Maria Josefa by nearly six years, to attend college and law school in Boston.[288]   Pedro ultimately became a ranchero in Santa Barbara, alcalde of Santa Barbara, and a member of the California State Assembly in 1854-1855.

Another friend of Tefft's was Capt. Henry Halleck, who gained fame later as the general-in-chief of all Union armies during the Civil War. Tefft became acquainted with Halleck during the Constitutional Convention. In a letter to Dana from Monterey on September 7, 1849, Tefft writes of Halleck, "Mr. Halleck's [sic] has been very kind indeed. I am still sleeping at Mr. Halleck's house – he is an excellent man and much esteemed here. He will, I hope, be the first governor of California under the new constitution."[289]   Halleck was acquainted with Dana. In a December 12, 1849, letter from Monterey, Tefft tells Dana, "Captain Halleck is well, sends his best regards …"[290]

Tragically, Tefft died just a year and a half after his wedding. On February 6, 1852, he was aboard the coastal steamer Ohio when it entered the harbor of Port San Luis amid high waves, heavy surf, and inclement weather. Tefft, reportedly planning to pick up Maria Josefa and then head on to San Francisco to take a train back to Wisconsin for a visit with his parents, insisted on going ashore. The captain sent Tefft and five sailors on a boat headed for shore. The roiling surf gave the men difficulty, and "within 100 yards of the sand … the boat suddenly turned over, dumping everyone into the pounding surf."[291]   Tefft and four of the sailors drowned. The heartbreaking incident impelled

Halleck to write Dana a letter of condolence on April 1, 1852. "Permit me, my dear sir, to offer to your family and to Mrs. Tefft, my deep sympathies in her bereavement; I knew the judge [Tefft] well, and had become attached to him by strong feelings of friendship and esteem and keenly regret his loss."[292]

During this time, Dana continued to extend hospitality to Yankees traveling through California. In March 1850, Dana hosted Charles Christopher Parry, the appointed botanist for the U.S. and Mexican boundary survey. At Rancho Nipomo, Parry collected a specimen of the pale-yellow layia, an annual herb native to California.[293] Dana also made the acquaintance of Henry Mellus, a future mayor of Los Angeles.[294]

* * *

Dana's confidence in American rule is reflected in his interest in being personally involved in the politics of his area. Under the short-lived military government of California, he served San Luis Obispo alcalde Miguel Avila beginning on May 22, 1849, as a sub-prefect, which included responsibilities as judge and inspector. Upon annexation, Dana organized two voting precincts in the San Luis Obispo district for California's first state election. One was located in his own home.

In that election, which was held November 13, 1849, Dana was dealt one of his first setbacks under Yankee rule when he ran for a State Senate seat in a district comprised of San Luis Obispo and Santa Barbara. The man elected,

Pablo de la Guerra of Santa Barbara, was able to win without receiving any votes in the San Luis Obispo district because the Santa Barbara district was so much more populous. In San Luis Obispo, Dana beat de la Guerra, 44-0. In Santa Barbara, however, de la Guerra led, 155-25, to win by an overall margin of 155-69. It has been alleged that Dana actually "received the largest vote ... but owing to imformalities [sic] in the election the office was accorded to Don Pablo de la Guerra, a native of California ... connected with one of the leading Spanish families of that country."[295]

No evidence can be found to substantiate the claim, but it is known that Dana did not find out the result of the election until some time after November 13. He wrote Joaquin Carrillo on November 16, "It is not only the right of the citizens of Santa Barbara, but of the whole state, to know why the returns of the election held here on the thirteenth have been so delayed. I have been in court several times, but not by examination among the inhabitants have I been able to find out the number of votes obtained by the various candidates in said election."[296] Dana continues, telling Carrillo in Spanish to "please send me a list of the votes given and for whom, also a list of the voters."[297] (Interestingly, Carrillo had been seated as the first county judge under American rule despite not knowing a word of English.)

Dana, whose name was recorded as "Denny" in the United States Census of 1850, was elected treasurer of San

Luis Obispo County in a general election held in September of that year. In May 1852, an act of legislature provided for boards of supervisors in each county. Dana initially was to be a county supervisor, but he was declared ineligible for that position because he also was county treasurer.[298] Later, Dana held the office of superintendent of county schools.[299] In 1857, Dana's son William Charles was elected county clerk of San Luis Obispo County at the age of 21.[300]

Nipomo:
A 'Most Horrid State'

Even with the economic prosperity associated with California's transition to American rule, Dana found life under the Stars and Stripes frustrating at times. To begin, he was disappointed with the American government's inability to help fight crime in San Luis Obispo and its environs.

To provide historical perspective, crime had been a worry for Dana and his neighbors since the 1840s. The area north of Dana's Nipomo ranch was well stocked with game and was often traveled by Native Americans from the Tulare Valley en route to forays upon the coast's great stock ranches. To fight off raids, it was necessary to arm and mount locals and "speed to the attack of the marauders."[301] Constant vigilance was required to protect the stock.

Ranchers in the vicinity of Nipomo also had problems with criminals passing through the area. "The *montes*, valleys and foothill passes of this part of California made good hiding places for all classes of rogues and the present Cuesta section was one of their favorite haunts," wrote Juan Francisco. "They also took to the sand dunes and shady canyons and no one felt safe when making a journey alone."[302]

Among the better-known criminals in the San Luis Obispo area during the mid-1840s were Pio Linares, Jack Powers, Joaquin Murrieta, Salomon Pico, Juan Soto, and Joaquin Valenzuela. Ironically, some of these men actually knew Dana or worked for him. Pio Linares was a vaquero who worked for Dana as a rider and trainer; according to Dana's son Juan Francisco, Linares "'broke' many horses for our family's use and a horse was fit for a queen to ride when he was through with it."[303]   Dana was apparently familiar with Jack Powers, a horseman and former U.S. soldier who unbeknownst to Dana and other locals was a notorious gambler and bandit. As Juan Francisco recounted, Powers tried to rob Dana's son Guillermo as Guillermo rode home with a large amount of cash from a cattle sale. Later, Powers visited Dana's home but found Guillermo safe and sound. Powers, who headed a gang of outlaws headquartered on the Nacimiento River north of San Luis Obispo, returned later with some accomplices. They fired several shots into the house and momentarily held the occupants of the house under siege. No one was hurt, and Powers finally drove off.[304]   Wrote Juan Francisco: "Some years later, at a Vigilante hanging in San Luis Obispo, some of Powers' men were brought before the Jury on various charges and some confessed to the raid upon Casa de Dana saying that Jack Powers had been their leader. At the time, though, none of us even suspected that Powers was a bandit."[305]

Aggravated by the crime wave in his area, Dana made an appeal to the military governor of California,

Colonel Richard B. Mason, on June 6, 1847, for military support for the alcalde of San Luis Obispo, Jose Mariano Bonilla. In Dana's words: "A military force absolutely necessary in the place. The Wild Indians are committing raids and carrying off droves of horses. Californians and foreigners formed a party and went after them – in a week return – found the Indians too strong – if some prompt measures are not adopted, the farmers will have to abandon their ranches."[306]   Dana continued, lamenting the state of society in San Luis Obispo. "Society is reduced here to the most horrid state. The whole place has for a long time past been a complete sink of drunkenness and debauchery. Alcalde's orders made nugatory, by want of force, to restore order. The more respectable reside on their farms at some distance from the mission, and it is morally impossible that they could unite [in case of an outbreak] in season, to be of any service."[307]

The crime troubles went on, as neither Mason nor the state government established after annexation offered any help to the San Luis Obispo authorities. Meanwhile, visiting Yankees caused disturbances in the area. Luganda Cota, a woman writing to Dana from Mission La Purisima on October 23, 1848, complained in Spanish that on "Saturday night the twenty-first of this month, there passed through here a group of foreign adventurers, who seek a crude form of fun. They wanted to break our doors down and finally robbed a horse … and also a mare … and, Jose having arrived, they took his horse, saddle and all and stole it."[308]   Cota continued, asking Dana to "do all possible to the end that these men deliver the beasts to my cousin Eugenio Lugo … and also the saddle to Don Jose."[309]   Dana responded immediately to Cota's request, ordering Don Joaquin Estrada the next day to "do everything" in Estrada's power to see that the stolen horses and saddle be delivered back to Cota.[310]

* * *

In addition to the problems with crime, Dana's land claim in Nipomo was adversely affected by the federal Land Act of 1851. Although the Treaty of Guadalupe Hidalgo that ended the Mexican War in 1848 stipulated that private property rights in Mexican territories such as California and New Mexico would be respected, the Land Act of 1851 was a blow to those like Dana who had received Mexican land grants. The legislation established a board of three land commissioners to review Mexican land grant claims and adjudicate them, and charged the United States Surveyor General with surveying confirmed land grants. In Dana's case, his land grant when surveyed measured 37,887.91 acres.[311]

Dana and his wife Maria Josefa referred to this in their last will, written in December 1853. In the document they state ownership of "six square Spanish leagues of land, more or less," which would have equaled roughly 34,500 acres.[312]   Nevertheless, some in the family continued to reference the original size of the land grant. Samuel A. Pollard referred to his father-in-law's "10 leagues" (nearly

60,000 acres) of land in an 1855 business proposal to Abel Stearns.[313]   In addition, according to family historian Alonzo Dana, Dana owned 1,400 acres south of San Luis Obispo in the area near what is now Tank Farm Road. This parcel, he ultimately gave to his daughter, Maria Josefa, who had recently married Pollard.[314]

* * *

A controversy over his "Casa Grande" building in which Dana became involved demonstrated how a Californianized American could end up in a legal battle with Americans new to the state. Dana rented the building to the county as a courthouse, and he fought with the county over the collection of rent. The controversy began in 1853 when Dana, in settling his accounts as county treasurer with the Court of Sessions, billed the county for the amount due for rent. Dana presented his bill for "rent of office from October, 1851, to October, 1853, at the rate of $12.50 per month; also rent of court room for twenty-eight days at $10.00 a day, the whole aggregating $580."[315] The Board of Supervisors ordered Dana at its meeting of February 1855 to release the county from his claim. But Dana did not comply with the order, and subsequently presented his bill for rent to the county in May of that year.

Dana's bill was rejected once more, and he filed suit against the county for payment. At the board's August 1855 meeting, the district attorney was ordered to defend the county. The records of the September session of the Board of Supervisors show that Dana won the suit. "It was ordered that a warrant be drawn in favor of Wm. G. Dana for the sum of $322.65, it being the amount of judgment and costs rendered by the District Court in his favor."[316] Thus the long dispute was ended in Dana's favor.

Dana, however, did not emerge from the drawn-out controversy untarnished. His predilection for the lifestyle of a *ranchero* surfaced when much was made of his "careless manner of doing business" as county treasurer.[317] A Board of Supervisors report of August 29, 1854, stated that "the late County Treasurer has kept no correct account of receipts or disbursements made by him during his term of office, and neglects, or is unable, to make the exhibit required by law."[318] One historian of the period wrote that "under the patriarchal habits of the principal families of the country," men such as Dana "had been accustomed to transact business loosely and unsystematically, but always attempting to deal fairly, keeping few accounts, and responsible to no one."[319]

Dana never had been much of an accountant. In a July 13, 1828, letter written to his friend John Rogers Cooper, he said that "as regards the accounts between us my time has been so much occupied that I have not even posted my books this two last months."[320] Nonetheless, the attention paid his lackluster accounting practices in 1854 indicated that a new order of things was coming into existence, one in which Dana would not necessarily feel comfortable. Juan Francisco wrote that "the older settlers of the country, like my father, were looked upon as 'one of the natives' because of their long residence and family ties in the country."[321]

There is much reason to think that Dana often felt like "one of the natives" when confronted with strict Yankee legalists seeking to enforce principles of accountability.

* * *

To combat his community's crime problems, Dana helped organize the San Luis Obispo County Vigilance Committee in 1858. The committee's charter document, signed on May 20 about three months after Dana's death, stated that its goal was "the repression and punishment of crime by all means whatsoever."[322] The Dana family also subscribed to the Vigilance Fund. Juan Francisco, still in his teens, was a member of the committee. "Most of the settlers around our part of the country ... believed in San Luis Obispo County and believed also that the Vigilante System was the only effective way to stop the crime wave. Every male citizen who obligated himself took on duties like those of a deputy sheriff."[323] The committee was eventually disbanded as opposition to it grew. Dana's role in the operation, however small, leaves one to observe that the quixotic California newcomer of the 1820s and 1830s could never have imagined that under Yankee rule crime control would entail a vigilance committee.

Dana's difficulties in American California are emblematic of frustrations felt by many following the change in regime. Opines Ferol Egan: "At first, it appeared that the discovery of gold in 1848 would simply add to the fortunes of the *rancheros*. Miners were more than willing to pay high prices for beef, horses, mules. Yet it was only a temporary affluence – and foreshadowed the collapse of a way of life. ... Legal contrivance, anti-Mexican attitudes ... brought the Age of the Californios to a close. Their languid culture simply collapsed beneath the weight of Yankee money, politics, and industrial power."[324]

* * *

Amid all of these developments, rheumatism so incapacitated Dana that he was confined in a state of paralysis to his house in the weeks leading up to his death at the age of 60 on February 12, 1858. "My father was very anxious to take part in business affairs when California became a part of the United States of his birth," wrote Juan Francisco, "but his long years at sea had left him with rheumatism that got worse as the years wore on. I remember in his last years on the Nipomo he became paralyzed and finally helpless and had to be a bystander in the events which were taking place and in which his older sons were taking part."[325] Likewise, Dana apparently regretted that he had not been even more immersed in the public affairs of the state. "After he retired to the rancho, he suffered so much [from rheumatism] that he could not take as active a part in public office in the new young state as he wished to do."[326]

Dana initially was buried in a hillside grave adjacent to his home, but later was moved to the Catholic Cemetery in San Luis Obispo, now called the Old Mission Cemetery. Maria Josefa lived 29 more years before following her husband in death on September 25, 1883. Before her passing, the rancho was divided into parcels so each son or daughter

**William Goodwin Dana's gravestone in
Old Mission Cemetery, San Luis Obispo**

or descendants would inherit a share.[327] Maria Josefa was buried with her husband in the Catholic Cemetery.

Dana and his wife now lie directly beneath a tall obelisk in the center of the Old Mission Cemetery. Their epitaphs are simple, listing merely their respective names, dates of birth, and dates of death. And yet the simplicity of Dana's burial site is deceiving. Dana is surrounded by family members, and adjacent headstones bear the last names of persons and families he knew, did business with, and influenced. He rests in a city in which he was a prominent public servant and entrepreneur, in a county he helped establish, and in a state that became part of the Union with some assistance by him. In his six decades Dana had gone from being an orphan to an adventurer to a fledgling settler to a respected public servant and businessman. William Goodwin Dana truly had been a man of consequence.

* * *

Dana's life, in the end, was a significant and historical one. It turns out that the man who was such a skilled navigator of sea vessels was even finer at navigating contrasting cultures. Moreover, his prescience about the opportunities available in California and his public service in his adopted land shows that his life was one of impact, of bold strokes, of resilience. Recounting his story, one can marvel at his sense of self-determination and efficacy. No matter how frustrated, disappointed, or depressed he may have been at various periods, he never sank into acquiescence or victimhood. No matter what challenge lie before him, Dana was a man who was ready to speak, to write, to decide, to plan, to act. As he himself wrote in one of his memorable missives to John Rogers Cooper, "To discourage me is no easy matter."

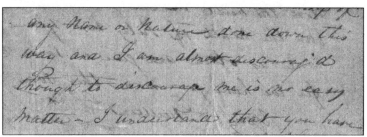

Excerpt from letter by William Goodwin Dana

APPENDIX I:
THE CAPTAIN TODAY

Today, over two centuries after his birth, the life of William Goodwin Dana resonates with those who know of him. Some are captivated by the Dana Adobe, his land holdings, and life at Rancho Nipomo. Some are fascinated by his encounters with famed historical figures such as John Fremont and Henry Halleck, and by the speculation over whether Dana ever crossed paths with his distant cousin Richard Henry. Some marvel at the many tales of Dana's hospitality, generosity, kindness, and decency. Some are interested, as is this book, in his ability to segue between juxtaposed American and Mexican cultures, Congregationalist and Catholic faiths, English and Spanish languages. Some – especially schoolchildren learning about Dana in preparation for a field trip to the adobe – cannot get over the size of Dana's family!

Happily, Dana's appeal is resulting in a widespread commitment to preserving his considerable legacy. In the past decade, an organization called the Dana Adobe Nipomo Amigos has worked extremely hard to restore Dana's home and to facilitate the purchase of neighboring properties. Now officially designated as a California Historic Landmark, the adobe and surrounding land one day will become a historical park replete with a museum, a visitor center, and a variety of attractions including a tall sycamore tree planted by Dana himself. Each year, a Rancho Nipomo Heritage Day is held that celebrates the life of Dana and his contemporaries. Meanwhile, an archaeological study is being done on the grounds of Dana's home; several people are working on historical research about his life, his family, and his land; and local historical societies are gathering documents and oral histories about Dana and his times. Dana's descendants have gotten into the act, holding reunions and helping with the restoration of the Dana Adobe. All of these efforts are serving to unite the residents of Nipomo and the Central Coast.

Perhaps the finest aspect of the current enthusiasm for Dana is that it is touching the hearts and minds of children. Children's books, works of historical fiction, and a play about Dana and Rancho Nipomo have been authored. A special children's day at the adobe this past summer drew well over 100 children. Close to a thousand students per year participate in field trips to the adobe, where they take tours of the house, make adobe bricks, learn to dance in the style of the ranchero period, and bake tortillas in an outdoor *horno*.

All of this is a fitting tribute to a man who was lauded by peers not just for his influence, but for his "respectability of character" and "good and honest intentions." William Goodwin Dana most certainly is a man worth studying, celebrating, and remembering … not just now, but for many decades to come.

APPENDIX II:
THE OFT-ASKED QUESTION

Richard Henry Dana's Two Years Before the Mast, an 1840 bestseller that gave a colorful account of a voyage around Cape Horn to California aboard the brig Pilgrim, has led many to reflect on the author's link to his California namesake. While Richard Henry and William Goodwin were related and both hailed from Boston, the men were fourth cousins. However, Richard Henry's description of an 1836 Santa Barbara wedding has sparked some speculation as to whether he snubbed his relative because of the severeness of William's change in lifestyle. The Pilgrim sailor's recounting of the January 10 nuptials of Alfred Robinson of Boston and Anita de la Guerra de Noriega y Carrillo does not mention William, a Santa Barbara resident who with his wife was "undoubtedly present at the wedding."[328]

There is room for conjecture in Richard Henry's omission of mention of Dana. Although both William and Richard Henry could trace their lineage to Richard Dana, the progenitor of the Dana family in America, one historian wonders whether William had not "cut himself off completely from his Boston relatives."[329] Elizabeth Ellery Dana, daughter of Richard Henry, has said "that as the Diary kept by her father on his voyage was destroyed,

Richard Henry Dana

he was forced to write his book from rough notes, and he may in this way have overlooked mention of his kinsman in Santa Barbara."[330] Richard Henry Dana III reportedly accounted for the omission "by referring to the difference in social status between William Dana, merchant of Santa Barbara, and Richard Henry, a mere sailor before the mast."[331] Juan Francisco Dana said that by "a quirk of fate," his father and Richard Henry did not even meet.[332]

A more interesting conclusion is that Richard Henry deliberately omitted Dana from his account because he was embarrassed by a family member's assimilation into Mexican society. The fuel for this argument is a description in the Russell Edition of Alfred Robinson's Life in California of Dana as "a native of Boston, captain of the schooner Waverly, said to be a blood-relation of Richard Henry Dana, and whom, it is also said, the latter refused to see when the Pilgrim anchored in the Puerto de Santa Barbara in January, 1835."[333] It has been written, moreover, that 19-year-old Richard Henry was a class-conscious Boston elitist who "could never let himself forget who he was and where he came from. ... Even in remote California the fact of being a Dana of Cambridge got him transferred to a ship returning earlier to the Atlantic coast. Two Years Before the Mast is shot through the anxiety of caste ... his perspective was that of a sojourner from above, ever on the edge of condescension. ... Falling deeper and deeper into the profanity and promiscuity of life as a sailor on the California coast, Dana fretted over loss of caste."[334] In that case, he might have felt that the Catholicized, Mexicanized Dana had by his actions disgraced his family.

Richard Henry Dana may have revealed his own feelings in a passage from Two Years Before the Mast. Writing of his visit to Monterey, he described what Americans needed to do in order to settle in California: "No Protestant has any political rights, nor can he hold property, or, indeed, remain more than a few weeks on shore, unless he belongs to a foreign vessel. Consequently, Americans and English who intend to reside here become Papists, the current phrase among them being: 'A man must leave his conscience at Cape Horn.'"[335] Later, detailing life in

Santa Barbara, Richard Henry Dana almost seems to be writing about William: "There are a number of English and Americans ... who have married Californians, become united to the Roman church, and acquired considerable property. Having more industry, frugality, and enterprise than the natives, they soon get nearly all the trade into their hands. ... The people are naturally suspicious of foreigners, and they would not be allowed to remain, were it not that they conform to the Church, and by marrying natives, and bringing up their children as Roman Catholics and Mexicans, and not teaching them the English language, they quiet suspicion, and even become popular and leading men. The chief alcaldes in Monterey and Santa Barbara were Yankees by birth."[336]

The Dana Family Tree

The relationship between Richard Henry Dana and Captain Dana

RICHARD DANA m.
b. 31 October 1617
Manchester, England
Arrived in New England
About 1640 (age 23)
d. April 2, 1690 in Cambridge

ANNE BULLARD
b. 1636 Watertown, Mass.
d. July 15, 1711, in Cambridge

Daniel m. Naomi Crosswell
b. 20 March 1663 in Cambridge
d. October 10, 1749

Benjamin m. Mary Buckminster
b. Feb. 20, 1660 in Cambridge
d. Feb. 14, 1754 in Newton, Mass.

Richard m. Lydia Trowbridge
b. June 26, 1700 in Boston
m. May 31, 1737 in Cambridge
d. May 17, 1772 in Boston

William m. Mary Greene
b. Sept. 12, 1703 in Boston
m. May 20, 1736 in Malden, Mass.
d. May 17, 1770 in Cambridge

Francis m. Elizabeth Ellery
b. June 13, 1743 in Charlestown
m. Aug. 5, 1775 in Cambridge
d. April 25, 1811 in Charlestown

Benjamin M. Lucy Whitney
b. April 6, 1741 in Cambridge
m. May 22, 1766 in Cambridge
d. before 1790

Richard Henry m.
Ruth Charlotte Smith
b. 1787 in Cambridge
m. about 1812 in Cambridge
d. 1879 in Cambridge

William m. Eliabeth Davis

b. 1767 in Watertown
m. Dec. 8, 1796 in Boston
d. June 3, 1799 in St. Thomas, WI

(author) Richard Henry Jr. m.	William Goodwin m.
Sarah Watson	Maria Josepha Carrillo
b. Aug. 1, 1815 in Cambridge	b. May 5, 1797
m. about 1840	m. Aug. 20, 1828 in Santa Barbara
d. Jan. 6, 1882 in Rome, Italy	d. Feb. 12, 1858 in Nipomo

NOTE: Richard Henry Dana, Jr., author of TWO YEARS BEFORE THE MAST, was a distant cousin of William Goodwin Dana. They both could trace their family tree back to Richard Dana who arived in New England about 1640. Richard Henry is descended from the line of Daniel, while William is descended through Daniel's brother, Benjamin. Also note that William Goodwin Dana was 18 years older than Richard Henry Dana, Jr.

WILLIAM G. DANA'S PARENTS & SISTER

PARENTS: William Dana and Elizabeth Davis
William Dana

> • Born in 1776 in Watertown and baptized in Newton Church
> • Married Elizabeth Davis, eldest daughter of Revolutionary officer Major Robert Davis in Boston on 8 December 1796
> • Died 3 June 1799 in St. Thomas, West Indies where he had gone for his health. A friend erected a stone in his memory

Elizabeth Davis

> • Born in 1778 in Boston. Her father was said to be one of the men in the Boston Tea Party
> • Married at 18 to William Dana in 1796
> • Two children:
> 1. William Goodwin Dana, born 5 May 1797 in Boston
> 2. Adeline Eliza Dana was born 12 June 1798 in Boston
> • Widowed at age 21 June 1799
> • Remarried at age 24 to Captain Thomas Chandler, Harvard graduate, in Worcester, Massachusetts on 25 December 1802. One child was born to this union, Theoda Chandler who died as a young child.
> • Widowed at age 26 when Chandler died on 13 May 1804
> • Remarried at age 27 to Captain James Rowan on 8 December 1805 in Boston
> • She died in Worcester at age 28 on 16 October 1806, leaving William age 9 and Adeline Eliza age 8.

SISTER: Adeline Eliza

> • Born 12 June 1798 in Boston, baptized at Second Church in Boston 1 July 1798
> • Married at age 31 to Reverend Charles Chauncy Darling, son of Doctor Samuel Darling of New Haven. on 28 July 1829 in Boston

- Died at age 84 in Saratoga, New York 11 September 1882
- Reverend Darling died in 1887
- Two sons: (nephews to William Dana)

Charles William Darling
- Born in New Haven on 11 October 1830
- Married Angeline Eliza Robertson
- Lived many years in Utica, New York
- Military engineer, attaining the position of Brig. General
- Life member of Oneida Historical Society. New York
- Secretary of Egypt Exploration Fund of London
- Member of Sons of the Revolutionary and Colonial Wars
- Died at country home in Asbury Park, New Jersey 22 June 1905

Elisha Colt Darling
- Born 25 February 1833 in New York City
- Died at age 18 on 13 July 1851

Note: Miniatures of Benjamin and Lucy Dana, painted by Malbone, were in possession of General Charles Darling who promised them to his California relatives, but they disappeared after his death.

APPENDIX III:
THE DANA–CARRILLO FAMILY

William Dana (1767-1799)

m.

Elizabeth Davis (1778-1806)

Captain William Dana (1797-1858)

Children/spouses

1. Maria Josefa (1829-1878)
   m. Henry Tefft (1 child)
   m. Samuel Pollard (5 children)
2. John (1830-1830)
3. Barbara (1831-1831)
4. Isabel (1832-1832)
5. Rosa (1833-1833)
6. Unnamed baby girl (1834-1834)
7. William Charles (1836-1898)
   m. Modesta Marie Castro (14 children)
8. Charles William (1837- ?)
   m. Blandina Refugio Esquer (8 children)
9. Juan Francisco (John Francis) (1838-1936)
   m. Francisca Thompson (10 children)
10. Henry Camilo (1839-1922)
    m. Josephine Blake (7 children)
11. Jose Ramon (1841-1919)
    m. Elena Francisca Streeter (6 children)

THE DANA–CARRILLO FAMILY (CONT.)

Carlos Antonio Carrillo (1783-1852)

m.

Maria Josefa Castro

Maria Josefa Carrillo (1812-1883)

---

12. Adelina Eliza (1842-1847)
13. Francis (Frank) (1843-?)
    m. Justina Clara Deleissigues (6 children)
14. Frederick (1844-1844)
15. Albert (1845-1845)
16. Edward Goodwin (1846-1917)
    m. Virginia Thorp Graves (8 children)
17. Adelina Eliza (1848-1924)
    m. Valentine Alviso (no children)
18. Frederick Albert (1849-1899)
    m. Manuela Tita Munoz (13 children)
19. David Amos (1851-1931)
    m. Cipriana Rojas (6 children)
20. Elisha Colt (1852-1914)
    m. Rosario De Soto (1 child)
21. Samuel Ambrose (1855-1924)
    m. Maria Antonio Alviso (no children)

APPENDIX IV:
RELATED PHOTOGRAPHS

Dana Adobe in 1960, prior to restoration

Volunteers making adobe bricks

A view of the Dana Adobe from its western entrance

**The view from the veranda includes the
Temetate Ridge of foothills**

A view of the Dana Adobe from the east

Captain and Mrs. Dana's bedroom has been restored

A Pacific Conservatory of Performing Arts (PCPA) actor
portrays William Goodwin Dana in Herb Kandel's 2004 play,
<u>Yankee Ciudadano: Sea Captain William Dana</u>
<u>Seeks His Dreams in Alta California</u>

BIBLIOGRAPHY

NON-FICTION

The most valuable and most enjoyable-to-read narrative on Dana forever will be Juan Francisco Dana's The Blond Ranchero. Other important accounts are Myron Angel's 1883 profile of Dana in his History of San Luis Obispo County, Helen Giffen's June 1937 article on Dana in the Southern California Quarterly, and Stephen Reynolds' journal detailing life in Honolulu in the 1820s. The source most revealing of Dana's own feelings is his own writing, numerous samples of which are at the Bancroft Library at the University of California at Berkeley and the Huntington Library in San Marino.

Angel, Myron. History of San Luis Obispo County, California, with Illustrations and Biographical Sketches of Its Prominent Men and Pioneers. Oakland, Calif.: Thompson & West, 1883.

Atherton, Faxon Dean. The California Diary of Faxon Dean Atherton, ed., Doyce B. Nunis Jr. San Francisco: California Historical Society, 1964.

Bancroft, Hubert Howe. The Works of Hubert Howe Bancroft, Vol. XIX, History of California, Vol. II 1801-1824. San Francisco: The History Company, Publishers, 1886.

Bancroft, Hubert Howe. The Works of Hubert Howe Bancroft, Vol. XX, History of California, Vol. III 1825-1840. San Francisco: The History Company, Publishers, 1886.

Beechey, Frederick William. Narrative of a Voyage to the Pacific and Beering's Strait: performed in His Majesty's ship. H. Colburn and R. Bentley, 1831.

Beidleman, Richard. California's Frontier Naturalists. Berkeley and Los Angeles: University of California Press, 2006.

Benefield, Hattie Stone. For the Good of the Country (Por el Bien del Pais): The Life Story, a Photo Album, and the Family Tree of William Benjamin Foxen. Los Angeles: Lorrin L. Morrison, Publisher, 1951.

Blomquist, Leonard Randolph. A Regional Study of the Changes in Life and Institutions in the San Luis Obispo District, 1830 to 1850. M.A. Thesis in History, University of California, October 1943.

Bryant, Edwin. What I Saw in California. Palo Alto, Calif.: Lewis Osborne, 1967.

Camp, Charles L. "The Chronicles of George C. Yount: California Pioneer of 1826." California Historical Society Quarterly, Vol. 2, No. 1, April 1923, pp. 3-66.

Carrillo, Leo. The California I Love: Leo Carrillo's Golden Cavalcade of California. Englewood Cliffs, N.J.: Prentice-Hall, 1961.

Dakin, Susanna Bryant. A Scotch Paisano in Old Los Angeles: Hugo Reid's Life in California, 1832-1852 Derived from His Correspondence. Berkeley and Los Angeles: University of California Press, 1939.

Dakin, Susanna Bryant. The Lives of William Hartnell. Stanford, Calif.: Stanford University Press, 1949.

Dana, Alonzo Patrick. California Pioneers: The Dana, Carrillo, Boronda, Deleissigues and Munoz Families in California, 1st ed. Arroyo Grande, Calif.: 1966.

Dana, Alonzo Patrick, as told to Doris Olsen. "Nipomo: Dana Family Made History." San Luis Obispo County Telegram-Tribune, March 22, 1976.

Dana, Alonzo Patrick. "The Beginning of Nipomo." Avila Beach Courier, undated.

Dana, Elizabeth Ellery. The Dana Family in America. Boston: Wright & Potter Printing Company, 1956.

Dana, Frank. "Frank Dana, Nipomo Rancho, 1840-1852." Nipomo News, July 22, 1892.

Dana, Frank. "Life on a Rancho." Nipomo News, July 1, 1892.

Dana, Frank. "The History of Nipomo." Nipomo News, June 4, 1892.

Dana, Frank. "What Was Life Like on a San Luis Obispo Rancho? How Did the Ranchero Make a Living?" Nipomo News, July 8, 1892.

Dana, Juan Francisco. The Blond Ranchero: Memories of Juan Francisco Dana, as told to Rocky Dana and Marie Harrington. Los Angeles: Dawson's Book Shop, 1960.

Dana, Juan Francisco. "Ten Decades on a California Rancho: Random Memories of Stirring Events in the Golden State Under Three Flags," as told to John Edwin Hogg. Touring Topics, Vol. 23, No. 11, November 1831, pp. 16-19, 44.

Dana, Richard Henry. Two Years Before the Mast: A Personal Narrative of Life at Sea. New York: Signet Classic, 2000 (originally published in 1840).

Dana, William G. Correspondence and Papers, 1827-1849. From the T.W. Norris Collection, Bancroft Library

Dana, William G. Diseño del Rancho Nipomo. Bancroft Library. From United States District Court, California, Southern District, Land Case 13.

Dana, William G., and Josefa Carrillo de Dana. Last Will and Testament. December 26, 1853.

Dana, William G. William G. Dana Papers, 1825-1858. Bancroft Library.

Dana, William G. Letter to Governor Mason, Nipomo, June 6, 1847. Unbound Documents, Archives of California, Vol. 63, p. 168.

Darling, Charles William. Memorial to My Fallen Kindred. Utica, N.Y.: Oneida Historical Society, 1888.

Davis, William Heath. Seventy-five Years in California, ed. Harold A. Small. San Francisco: John Howell Books, 1967.

de la Cuesta, Tulita. "The Story of a Table and a Wreck in 1849 of the Steamer Edith off Rocky Point Arguello." Santa Ynez Valley News, September 17, 1954.

Documentos Para la Historia de California, Vol. 29 1826-1829. Archive of Don Mariano Guadalupe Vallejo, presented to the Bancroft Library, 1874.

Documentos Para la Historia de California, Vol. 30 1830-1832. Archive of Don Mariano Guadalupe Vallejo, presented to the Bancroft Library, 1874.

"Dr. John S. Griffin's Mail, 1846-53", ed. Viola Lockhart Warren. California Historical Society Quarterly, Vol. 33, No. 4, December 1954, pp. 337-347.

Egan, Ferol. "Twilight of the Californios." The American West, Vol. 6, No. 2, March 1969.

Engelhardt, Zephyrin. Mission San Diego. San Francisco: The James H. Barry Company, 1920.

Evans, George W. B. Mexican Gold Trail: The Journal of a Forty-Niner. San Marino, Calif.: The Huntington Library, 1945.

Fremont, John Charles. The Expeditions of John Charles Fremont: Volume 2: The Bear Flag Revolt and the Court-Martial, eds. Donald Jackson and Mary Lee Spence. Urbana, Ill.: University of Illinois Press, 1973.

Galvin, John, ed. The Coming of Justice to California, translated from Spanish by Adelaide Smithers. San Francisco: John Howell Books, 1963.

Gates, Paul W. "The Land Business of Thomas O. Larkin," California Historical Quarterly, Vol. 54, No. 4, Winter 1975, pp. 323-344.

Giffen, Guy J., and Helen S. Giffen. "Tracing Fremont's Route with the California Battalion from San Juan Bautista to Los Angeles, November, 1846 to January, 1847." Southern California Quarterly, Vol. 19, No. 2, June 1937, pp. 49-62.

Giffen, Helen S. "An Adopted Californian: The Life and Letters of William Goodwin Dana." Southern California Quarterly, Vol. 19, No. 2, June 1937, pp. 49-62.

Greer, Richard A. "Notes on Early Land Title and Tenure in Hawaii." The Hawaiian Journal of History, Vol. 30, 1996.

Haase, Ynez. "The Middle of Nowhere: The Carlos Carrillo Adobe, the Carrillo Family, & Their Rancho Sespe." The Ventura County Historical Society Quarterly, Vol. 45, No. 2, 2001.

Hall-Patton, Mark. "Going to Goleta: Historical Trip South Includes Practical Joker." South County Tribune, March 24, 1988.

Halleck, Peachy, & Billings Records, 1852-1867. Bancroft Library.

Hammatt, Charles H. Ships, Furs, and Sandalwood: A Yankee Trader in Hawaii, 1823-1825. Honolulu: University of Hawaii Press, 1999.

Harlow, Neal. California Conquered: The Annexation of a Mexican Province, 1846-1850. Berkeley and Los Angeles: University of California Press, 1982.

Hawgood, John A. "The Pattern of Yankee Infiltration in Mexican Alta California, 1821-1846." Pacific Historical Review, Vol. 27, No. 1, February 1958, pp. 27-37.

Hill, Lawrence, and Marion Parks, eds. Santa Barbara, Tierra Adorada: A Community History. Los Angeles: Security-First National Bank of Los Angeles, 1930.

Hoover, Mildred Brooke, Ethel Grace Rensch, and Hero Eugene Rensch, eds.; revised by Ruth Teiser. Historic Spots in California. Palo Alto, Calif.: Stanford University Press, 1948.

Hutton, William Rich. Glances at California 1847-1853: Diaries and Letters of William Rich Hutton. San Marino, Calif.: The Huntington Library, 1942.

"Journal of John McHenry Hollingsworth." California Historical Society Quarterly, Vol. 1, No. 3, January 1923, pp. 207-270.

Kirker, Harold. California's Architectural Frontier: Style and Tradition in the Nineteenth Century. San Marino, Calif.: The Huntington Library, 1960.

Kirker, Harold. "The Role of Hispanic Kinships in Popularizing the Monterey Style in California, 1836-1846." Journal of the Society of Architectural Historians, Vol. 48, No. 3, October 1984, pp. 250-251.

Kuykendall, Ralph S. The Hawaiian Kingdom, 1778-1854. Honolulu: University of Hawaii Press, 1947.

The Larkin Papers: Personal, Business, and Official Correspondence of Thomas Oliver Larkin, Merchant and United States Consul in California, ed. George P. Hammond. Bancroft Library.

Martin, Thomas Salathiel. With Fremont: To California and the Southwest, 1845-1849, ed. Ferol Egan. Aptos, Calif.: Grace Hoper Press, 1975.

McLane, Louis. The Private Journal of Louis McLane, USN, 1844-1848, ed. Jay Monahan. Los Angeles: Dawson's Book Shop, 1971.

McWilliams, Carey. North from Mexico: The Spanish-Speaking People of the United States. New York: Monthly Review Press, 1961.

Mission Santa Ines, Record of Deaths.

Monroy, Thomas. Thrown Among Strangers: The Making of Mexican Culture in Frontier California. Berkeley: University of California Press, 1990.

Morrison, Mrs. Annie L., and John H. Haydon. History of San Luis Obispo County and Environs. Los Angeles: Historic Record Company, 1917.

Native Register: The Department of Land and Natural Resources Board of Commissioners to Quiet Land Title, translated by Frances Fazier. Honolulu: Hawaii State Archives, 1976. Vols. 1-9 Microfilm S01755, Reel 1.

Nidever, George. Life and Adventures of George Nidever, ed. William Henry Ellison. Berkeley, Calif.: University of California Press, 1937.

Nipomo Rancho: Santa Barbara and San Luis Obispo Counties, Expediente No. 25, Spanish Archives. From California State Archives, Sacramento. Compiled for Los Californianos by Charmaine A. Burdell, Myrtle G. Jewett, and Eleanor and Ben Sargis.

Norton, Gladys. "Our Dana Adobe." Article published by San Luis Obispo County Historical Society, January 1956.

Ogden, Adele. "Alfred Robinson, New England Merchant in Mexican California." California Historical Society Quarterly, Vol. 23, No. 3, September 1944, pp. 193-218.

Ogden, Adele. The California Sea Otter Trade 1784-1848. Berkeley and Los Angeles: University of California Press, 1941.

Ogden, Adele. Trading Vessels on the California Coast, 1786-1848. California State Library, 1979 (microfilm).

Older, Fremont. Love Stories of Old California. Freeport, N.Y.: Books for Libraries Press, 1940.

Osio, Antonio Maria. The History of Alta California: A Memoir of Mexican California, translated by Rose Marie Beebe and Robert M. Senkewicz. Madison, Wis.: The University of Wisconsin Press, 1996.

Paulding, Ruth. "Captain William Goodwin Dana." Presentation given to children, March 1972. Transcribed by Jean Hubbard for San Luis Obispo County Historical Society.

Pitt, Leonard. The Decline of the Californios: A Social History of the Spanish-Speaking Californians, 1846-1890. Berkeley and Los Angeles: University of California Press, 1968.

Pourade, Richard. Time of the Bells. San Diego: Union-Tribune Publishing Company, Copley Press, 1961.

Reynolds, Stephen. Journal of Stephen Reynolds: Vol. I, 1823-1829, ed. Pauline N. King. Salem, Mass.: The Peabody Museum of Salem, 1989.

Robinson, Alfred. Life in California Before the Conquest, ed. Thomas C. Russell. San Francisco: The Private Press of Thomas C. Russell, 1925.

Robinson, W.W. The Story of San Luis Obispo County. San Luis Obispo, Calif.: Title Insurance and Trust Company, 1957.

Rogers, Fred B. "Bear Flag Lieutenant: The Life Story of Henry L. Ford." California Historical Society Quarterly, Vol. 29, No. 4, December 1950, pp. 333-344.

Rogers, Fred B. Bear Flag Lieutenant: The Life Story of Henry L. Ford. San Francisco: California Historical Society, 1951.

Rolle, Andrew F. An American in California: The Biography of William Heath Davis, 1822-1909. San Marino, Calif.: Huntington Library, 1956.

Rolle, Andrew F. "The Riddle of Jedediah Smith's First Visit to California." Southern California Quarterly, Vol. 36, No. 3, September 1954, pp. 179-184.

Rubcic, Michael A. "An Appraisal of the David Dana Ranch Nipomo, California." B.S. senior project, presented to the faculty of the Agricultural Management Department, California Polytechnic State University, San Luis Obispo, March 1981.

Sarah (last name unknown). Letter to William G. Dana. January 6, 1821.

Sherman, General William T. "Old Times in California." The North American Review, Vol. 148, No. 388, March 1889.

Simpson, Sir George. Voyages to California Ports, 1841-42. San Francisco: The Private Press of Thomas C. Russell, 1930.

Spanish and Mexican Land Grant Maps, 1855-1875. California State Archives. From the United States Surveyor General for California.

Starr, Kevin. Americans and the California Dream 1850-1915. Santa Barbara and Salt Lake City: Peregrine Smith, Inc.: 1981.

Stearns (Abel) Papers, Collection I. Huntington Library.

Stewart, Charles Samuel. Journal of a Residence in the Sandwich Islands During the Years 1823, 1824, and 1825. Boston: Weeks, Jordan & Company, 1839.

Storke, Yda Addis. A Memorial and Biographical History of the Counties of Santa Barbara, San Luis Obispo and Ventura, California. Chicago: The Lewis Publishing Company, 1891.

Streeter, William A. "Recollections of Historical Events in California, 1843-1878," ed. William Henry Ellison. California Historical Society Quarterly, Vol. 18, No. 2, June 1939, pp. 157-179.

Tefft, Thomas R. "Episodes from the Short, Happy Life of Henry Tefft." The Californians, Vol. 10, No. 2, September/October 1992, pp. 34-39.

Tennis, George. "California's First State Election November 13, 1849." Southern California Quarterly, Vol. 50, No. 4, December 1968, pp. 357-394.

Thomes, William H. On Land and Sea, or California in the Years 1843, '44, and '45. Boston: DeWolfe, Fiske & Company, 1884.

Tompkins, Walker A. It Happened in Old Santa Barbara. Santa Barbara, Calif.: Santa Barbara National Bank, 1976.

Tompkins, Walker A. Santa Barbara History Makers. Goleta, Calif.: Kimberly Press, 1983.

Tompkins, Walker A. Santa Barbara's Royal Rancho: The Fabulous History of Los Dos Pueblos. Berkeley: Howell-North Books, 1960.

Walker, Judy. "The Historical Heritage of Nipomo." B.A. senior project, presented to the faculty of the History Department, California Polytechnic State University, San Luis Obispo, August 1965.

Woodward, Arthur. "Sea Otter Hunting on the Pacific Coast." Southern California Quarterly, Vol. 20, No. 3, September 1938, pp. 119-134.

Woolfenden, John, and Amelie Elkington. Cooper: Juan Bautista Rogers Cooper, Sea Captain, Adventurer, Ranchero, and Early California Pioneer, 1791-1872. Pacific Grove, Calif.: The Boxwood Press, 1983.

"Yerba Buena Biographies." California Historical Society Quarterly, Vol. 14, No. 2, June 1935, pp. 123-131.

FICTION

Some works of children's historical fiction have been based on Dana and life at Rancho Nipomo.

Faber, Gail, and Michelle Lasagna. Clara Rides the Rancho. Alamo, Calif.: Magpie Publications, 2001.

Porter, Wanda. Sister Sara. Nipomo, Calif.: Dana Adobe Nipomo Amigos, 2002.

Porter, Wanda. <u>Blanco</u>. Nipomo, Calif.: Dana Adobe Nipomo Amigos, 2003.

Porter, Wanda. <u>Emily Decides</u>. Nipomo, Calif.: Dana Adobe Nipomo Amigos, 2002.

Rubcic, Michael. <u>Native Soul</u>. Summerland, Calif.: Native Sun Press, 2004.

A play by the Pacific Conservatory of Performing Arts was based on the life of Dana and his romance with Maria Josefa Carrillo.

Kandel, Herb. <u>Yankee Ciudadano</u>. Performed by Pacific Conservatory of Performing Arts Outreach Program, 2004-2005.

NOTES

1. Elizabeth Ellery Dana, The Dana Family in America (Boston: Wright & Potter Printing Company, 1956), p. 36.

2. Charles William Darling, Memorial to My Fallen Kindred (Utica, N.Y.: Oneida Historical Society, 1888), p. 101.

3. Elizabeth Ellery Dana, p. 312.

4. Ibid.

5. Myron Angel, History of San Luis Obispo County, California, with Illustrations and Biographical Sketches of Its Prominent Men and Pioneers (Oakland, Calif.: Thompson & West, 1883), p. 102.

6. Adeline E. Dana, letter to William G. Dana, December 29, 1825, in William G. Dana Papers, 1825-1858 (Bancroft Library).

7. Andrew F. Rolle, An American in California: The Biography of William Heath Davis, 1822-1909 (San Marino, Calif.: Huntington Library, 1956), p. 6.

8. Ibid., pp. 6-7.

9. Ibid., p. 6.

10. Richard Pourade, Time of the Bells (San Diego: Union-Tribune Publishing Company, Copley Press, 1961), "Chapter 8: The Boston Ships."

11. Helen S. Giffen, "An Adopted Californian: The Life and Letters of William Goodwin Dana," Southern California Quarterly, Vol. 19, No. 2, June 1937, p. 50.

12. Sarah (last name unknown), letter to William G. Dana, January 6, 1821.

13. Ibid.

14. Ibid.

15. Giffen, p. 50.

16. Ibid.

17. Richard A. Greer, "Notes on Early Land Title and Tenure on Hawaii," The Hawaiian Journal of History, Vol. 30, 1996.

18. Rolle, pp. 6-7.

19. According to missionary Elisha Loomis, Davis "literally killed himself with strong drink." From Rolle, p. 7.

20. Angel, p. 103.

21. Ralph S. Kuykendall, The Hawaiian Kingdom, 1778-1854 (Honolulu: University of Hawaii Press, 1947), p. 95.

22. Charles H. Hammatt, Ships, Furs, and Sandalwood: A Yankee Trader in Hawaii, 1823-1825 (Honolulu: University of Hawaii Press, 1999), p. 40.

23. Charles Samuel Stewart, Journal of a Residence in the Sandwich Islands During the Years 1823, 1824, and 1825 (Boston: Weeks, Jordan & Company, 1839), p. 204.

24. "Yerba Buena Biographies", California Historical Society Quarterly, Vol. 14, No. 2, June 1935, p. 127.

25. Stephen Reynolds, Journal of Stephen Reynolds: Vol. I, 1823-1829, ed. Pauline N. King (Salem, Mass.: The Peabody Museum of Salem, 1989), p. xii.

26. Rolle, p. 8.

27. Reynolds, pp. 5, 21.

28. Ibid., p. 5.

29. Ibid., p. 7.

30. Ibid., p. 8.

31. Ibid.

32. Ibid., p. 11.

33. Ibid., p. 14.

34. Ibid.

35. Ibid., p. 15.

36. Ibid., p. 19.

37. Ibid., p. 21.

38. Ibid., p. 118.

39. Ibid., p. 119.

40. Ibid., pp. 120, 122.

41. Ibid., p. 127.

42.   Ibid.
43.   Ibid., p. 12.
44.   Ibid., p. 17.
45.   Ibid., p. 119.
46.   Ibid., p. 10.
47.   Ibid., p. 18.
48.   Ibid., p. 20.
49.   Ibid., p. 21.
50.   Ibid., p. 52.
51.   Ibid., p. 76.
52.   Adeline E. Dana, letter to William G. Dana, December 29, 1825, William G. Dana Papers, 1825-1858.
53.   Ibid.
54.   Reynolds., p. 140.
55.   Angel, p. 102.
56.   Ibid.
57.   Walker A. Tompkins, Santa Barbara History Makers (Goleta, Calif.: Kimberly Press, 1983), pp. 41-44.
58.   Pourade, "Chapter 8: The Boston Ships."
59.   The bill of lading was written on October 22, 1826. Angel, p. 103.
60.   Reynolds, p. 133.
61.   Ibid., pp. 134-135.
62.   Ibid., p. 136.
63.   Ibid.
64.   Ibid., p. 137.
65.   Ibid.
66.   Ibid., pp. 137-138.
67.   Ibid., p. 173.
68.   Ibid.
69.   Ibid.
70.   Ibid.
71.   Ibid., p. 175.

72. Native Register: The Department of Land and Natural Resources of Commissioners to Quiet Land Title, translated by Frances Fazier (Honolulu: Hawaii State Archives, 1976), Vols. 1-9, Microfilm S01755, Reel 1, p. 178.
73. Ibid, p. 185.
74. Ibid.
75. Ibid.
76. Ibid.
77. Ibid., p. 79.
78. Ibid., p. 209.
79. Ibid.
80. Ibid, p. 210.
81. Ibid.
82. Ynez Haase, "The Middle of Nowhere: The Carlos Carrillo Adobe, the Carrillo Family, & Their Rancho Sespe," The Ventura County Historical Society Quarterly, Vol. 45, No. 2, 2001, p. 35.
83. Zephyrin Engelhardt, San Diego Mission (San Francisco: The James H. Barry Company, 1920), pp. 281, 283.
84. Richard Henry Dana, Two Years Before the Mast: A Personal Narrative of Life at Sea (New York: Signet Classic, 2000; originally published in 1840), p. 50.
85. Sir George Simpson, Voyages to California Ports, 1841-42 (San Francisco: The Private Press of Thomas C. Russell, 1930).
86. John Woolfenden and Amelie Elkington, Cooper: Juan Bautista Rogers Cooper, Sea Captain, Adventurer, Ranchero, and Early California Pioneer, 1791-1872 (Pacific Grove, Calif.: The Boxwood Press, 1983), p. 9-11.
87. Ibid., p. 9.
88. Ibid., p. 33.
89. William G. Dana, letter to John R. Cooper, January 5, 1827, in Documentos Para la Historia de California, Vol. 29 1826-1829 (Archive of Don Mariano Guadalupe Vallejo, presented to the Bancroft Library, 1874).

90. William G. Dana, letter to John R. Cooper, November 6, 1827, Vallejo Documents, Vol. 29.
91. Ibid.
92. Ibid.
93. William G. Dana, letter to John R. Cooper, Santa Barbara, May 12, 1828, Vallejo Documents, Vol. 29.
94. Ibid.
95. William G. Dana, letter to John R. Cooper, San Buenaventura, July 13, 1828, Vallejo Documents, Vol. 29.
96. Angel, p. 103.
97. Ibid.
98. Woolfenden and Elkington, p. 51.
99. Haase, p. 46.
100. Juan Francisco Dana, The Blond Ranchero: Memories of Juan Francisco Dana, as told to Rocky Dana and Marie Harrington (Los Angeles: Dawson's Book Shop, 1960), p. 15.
101. Ibid.
102. Reynolds, p. 237.
103. Giffen, p. 52.
104. Ibid., pp. 52-53.
105. Woolfenden and Elkington, p. 33.
106. Benefield, For the Good of the Country (Por el Bien del Pais): The Life Story, a Photo Album, and the Family Tree of William Benjamin Foxen (Los Angeles: Lorrin L. Morrison, Publisher, 1951), p. 14.
107. Walker A. Tompkins, Santa Barbara's Royal Rancho: The Fabulous History of Los Dos Pueblos (Berkeley: Howell-North Books, 1960), p. 51.
108. William G. Dana, letter to John R. Cooper, Santa Barbara, May 12, 1828, Vallejo Documents, Vol. 29.
109. William G. Dana, letter to John R. Cooper, San Buenaventura, July 13, 1828, Vallejo Documents, Vol. 29.

110. William G. Dana, letter to John R. Cooper, Santa Barbara, October 28, 1828, Vallejo Documents, Vol. 29.
111. William G. Dana, letter to John R. Cooper, Santa Barbara, June 25, 1830, in Documentos Para la Historia de California, Vol. 30 1830-1832 (Archive of Don Mariano Guadalupe Vallejo, presented to the Bancroft Library, 1874).
112. Reynolds, p. 252.
113. Ibid., p. 253.
114. Ibid., p. 258.
115. Ibid., p. 260.
116. Thomas Monroy, Thrown Among Strangers: The Making of Mexican Culture in Frontier California (Berkeley: University of California Press, 1990), p. 156.
117. Ibid.
118. Ibid.
119. William G. Dana, letter to Abel Stearns, April 1, 1833, Stearns (Abel) Papers, Collection I, Huntington Library.
120. Healthy Hawaiian men were recruited to serve on ships that came to and from Hawaii. By the late 1840s, the Hawaiian government took action to protect native men by requiring ship captains to post bonds for the safe return of the native sailors.
121. William G. Dana, letter to Abel Stearns, April 1, 1833, Stearns (Abel) Papers, Collection I, Huntington Library.
122. Ibid.
123. William G. Dana, letter to Abel Stearns, December 17, 1838, Stearns (Abel) Papers, Collection I, Huntington Library.
124. William G. Dana, letter to Abel Stearns, undated, Stearns (Abel) Papers, Collection I, Huntington Library.
125. Ibid.
126. William G. Dana, letter to Abel Stearns, 1836, Stearns (Abel) Papers, Collection I, Huntington Library.
127. William G. Dana, letter to Abel Stearns, 1836, Stearns (Abel) Papers, Collection I, Huntington Library.

128. William G. Dana, letter to Abel Stearns, July 7, 1836, Stearns (Abel) Papers, Collection I, Huntington Library.

129. Ibid.

130. Ibid.

131. Tompkins, pp. 41-44.

132. William G. Dana, letter to Abel Stearns, February 27, 1836, Stearns (Abel) Papers, Collection I, Huntington Library.

133. Ibid.

134. Ibid.

135. William G. Dana, letter to Abel Stearns, March 4, 1836, Stearns (Abel) Papers, Collection I, Huntington Library. "Chin Chin" was a Chinese pidgin English phrase meaning "farewell".

136. William G. Dana, letter to Abel Stearns, December 17, 1838, Stearns (Abel) Papers, Collection 1.

137. Although Dana complained about bad debts, he may have defaulted on some personal loans himself. In a May 1846 letter to U.S. Consul Thomas O. Larkin regarding the death of a William Smith in Sonoma, Jacob Primer Leese wrote, "The old Man [Smith] has I beleav no property what ever in this Cunterey … I hav often heard the old man say that Mr Wm Daney of Santa Barbara is owing him Three hundred Dollars." From The Larkin Papers: Personal, Business, and Official Correspondence of Thomas Oliver Larkin, Merchant and United States Consul in California, ed. George P. Hammond, Vol. IV, October 1, 1845-May 31, 1846, pp. 364-365.

138. Tompkins, pp. 65-66.

139. Arthur Woodward, "Sea Otter Hunting on the Pacific Coast," Southern California Quarterly, Vol. 20, No. 3, September 1938, p. 126.

140. Adele Ogden, The California Sea Otter Trade 1784-1848 (Berkeley and Los Angeles: University of California Press, 1941), p. 106.

141. Ibid.

142. Ibid., p. 108.
143. Charles L. Camp, "The Chronicles of George C. Yount: California Pioneer of 1826," California Historical Society Quarterly, Vol. 2, No. 1, April 1923, p. 45.
144. Ibid., p. 46.
145. Ibid.
146. George Nidever, The Life and Adventures of George Nidever, ed. William Henry Ellison (Berkeley: University of California Press, 1937), p. 36.
147. Ibid., pp. 39-40.
148. Ibid., p. 46.
149. Ibid., p. 49.
150. Ogden, p. 113.
151. Andrew F. Rolle, "The Riddle of Jedediah Smith's First Visit to California," Southern California Quarterly, Vol. 36, No. 3, September 1954, p. 181.
152. Juan F. Dana, pp. 76, 119.
153. Ibid., pp. 35-37.
154. Tompkins, p. 57.
155. Benefield, p. 7.
156. Mark Hall-Patton, "Going to Goleta: Historical Trip South Includes Practical Joker," South County Tribune, March 24, 1988.
157. "Jack Mitchener came fro Ranai in Sch. Medford with old copper & iron from wreck of ship London for Mr. Dana, 10 piculs old copper, 16 piculs iron bolts, twenty three Deadeyes & straps – 2 piculs lead Some plank & c." Reynolds, pp. 140-141.
158. Ibid.
159. William G. Dana, letter to John R. Cooper, Santa Barbara, June 20, 1829, Vallejo Documents, Vol. 29.
160. Juan F. Dana, pp. 35-37.
161. Ibid., p. 38.
162. Ibid., p. 37.

163. William G. Dana, letter to John R. Cooper, Santa Barbara, June 25, 1830, Vallejo Documents, Vol. 30.

164. Interestingly, Dana and Maria Josefa drew from both Mexican and American cultures in naming their children. Refer to Appendix on Dana-Carrillo Family. From Alonzo Patrick Dana, California Pioneers: The Dana, Carrillo, Boronda, Deleissigues and Munoz Families in California, 1st ed. (Arroyo Grande, California: 1966), pp. 25-32.

165. William G. Dana, letter to John R. Cooper, Santa Barbara, June 20, 1859, Vallejo Documents, Vol. 29.

166. John Galvin, ed., The Coming of Justice to California, translated from Spanish by Adelaide Smithers (San Francisco: John Howell Books, 1963).

167. Haase, p. 6.

168. Juan F. Dana, p. 107.

169. The house no longer exists, but its location is just south of the Presidio on what is now Cañon Perdido Street.

170. Nipomo Rancho: Santa Barbara and San Luis Obispo Counties, Expediente No. 25, Spanish Archives, from California State Archives, Sacramento (compiled for Los Californianos by Charmaine A. Burdell, Myrtle G. Jewett, and Eleanor and Ben Sargis), p. 1.

171. Ibid.

172. William G. Dana, Diseño del Rancho Nipomo, Bancroft Library, from United States District Court, California, Southern District, Land Case 13.

173. Nipomo Rancho: Santa Barbara and San Luis Obispo Counties, Expediente No. 25, Spanish Archives, p. 1.

174. Ibid., pp. 2-3.

175. Ibid., p. 3.

176. Ibid.

177. Ibid.

178. Ibid., p. 6.

179. Ibid., p. 9.
180. Alonzo Patrick Dana, as told to Doris Olsen, "Nipomo: Dana Family Made History," San Luis Obispo County Telegram-Tribune, March 22, 1976.
181. Juan F. Dana, p. 16.
182. Ibid., pp. 16-17.
183. Frank Dana, "The History of Nipomo", Nipomo News, June 4, 1892.
184. Harold Kirker, California's Architectural Frontier: Style and Tradition in the Nineteenth Century (San Marino, Calif.: The Huntington Library, 1960), p. 16.
185. Ibid.
186. Juan F. Dana, p. 13.
187. Ibid., p. 18.
188. Ibid., pp. 109, 113.
189. Mildred Brooke Hoover, Ethel Grace Rensch, and Hero Eugene Rensch, eds., revised by Ruth Teiser, Historic Spots in California (Palo Alto, Calif.: Stanford University Press, 1948), p. 302. Cave Landing is located adjacent to Pirate's Cove, a secluded site that for decades has been a clothing-optional beach.
190. Juan F. Dana, p. 83.
191. Frank Dana, "Life on a Rancho," Nipomo News, July 1, 1892.
192. Ruth Paulding, "Captain William Goodwin Dana" (presentation given to children, March 1972; transcribed by Jean Hubbard for San Luis Obispo County Historical Society).
193. Rolle, p. 46.
194. Juan F. Dana, p. 114.
195. Ibid., p. 21.
196. Ibid., p. 18.
197. Ibid., p. 21.
198. Ferol Egan, "Twilight of the Californios," The American West, Vol. 6, No. 2, March 1969, pp. 1-4.

199. Reynolds, p. 10. "Fine day – attended meeting all day – several Americans at morning service three or four at English – afternoon – Mr Jones, Dana, Green, Temple & self Capt Sturgis, Grymes & Clark were at meeting."

200. Faxon Dean Atherton, The California Diary of Faxon Dean Atherton, ed., Doyce B. Nunis Jr. (San Francisco: California Historical Society, 1964), p. 88.

201. Ibid., pp. 88-89.

202. Ibid., p. 89.

203. Mission Santa Ines, Record of Deaths, Listing No. 2787.

204. Juan F. Dana, p. 50.

205. Ibid., pp. 50-51.

206. Angel, p. 104.

207. Ibid.

208. Ibid., p. 105.

209. Antonio Maria Osio, The History of Alta California: A Memoir of Mexican California, translated by Rose Marie Beebe and Robert M. Senkewicz (Madison, Wis.: The University of Wisconsin Press, 1996), pp. 190-191.

210. Juan F. Dana, pp. 77-78.

211. Angel, p. 105.

212. William Heath Davis, Seventy-five Years in California, ed. Harold A. Small (San Francisco: John Howell Books, 1967), p. 292.

213. Ibid., p. 95.

214. Ibid.

215. Ibid., p. 96.

216. William A. Streeter, "Recollections of Historical Events in California, 1843-1878," ed. William Henry Ellison, California Historical Society Quarterly, Vol. 18, No. 2, June 1939, p. 163.

217. Ibid.

218. Ibid.

219. Guy J. Giffen and Helen S. Giffen, "Tracing Fremont's Route with the California Battalion from San Juan Bautista to Los Angeles, November, 1846 to January, 1847," Southern California Quarterly, Vol. 22, No. 1, March 1940, pp. 14-15.

220. Ibid., p. 15.

221. Ibid.

222. Benefield, p. 42.

223. Ibid.

224. Juan F. Dana, pp. 23-24.

225. Ibid.

226. Edwin Bryant, What I Saw in California (Palo Alto, Calif.: Lewis Osborne, 1967), p. 377.

227. Juan F. Dana, p. 25.

228. Ibid. According to Juan Francisco, his father never did redeem the payment.

229. Ibid.

230. Ibid.

231. Ibid., pp. 27-28.

232. Ibid., pp. 25-26.

233. Bryant, p. 423.

234. Louis McLane, The Private Journal of Louis McLane, USN, 1844-1848, ed. Jay Monahan (Los Angeles: Dawson's Book Shop, 1971).

235. Juan F. Dana, p. 26.

236. Ibid.

237. Ibid., pp. 26-27.

238. Ibid., p. 27.

239. Ibid.

240. "Journal of John McHenry Hollingsworth," California Historical Society Quarterly, Vol. 1, No. 3, January 1923, p. 263.

241. "Dr. John S. Griffin's Mail, 1846-53," ed. Viola Lockhart Warren, California Historical Society Quarterly, Vol. 33, No. 4, December 1954, pp. 342-344.

242. Ibid.

243. Angel, p. 105.

244. General William T. Sherman, "Old Times in California," The North American Review, Vol. 148, No. 388, March 1889, p. 271.

245. Juan F. Dana, p. 29.

246. Ibid., p. 31.

247. Angel, pp. 102-103.

248. Giffen, p. 57.

249. Ibid., p. 60.

250. Juan F. Dana, p. 68.

251. Ibid.

252. Judy Walker, "The Historical Heritage of Nipomo," (B.A. senior project, presented to the faculty of the History Department, California Polytechnic State University, San Luis Obispo, August 1965), p. 23.

253. Paulding.

254. Tulita de la Cuesta, "The Story of a Table and a Wreck in 1849 of the Steamer Edith off Rocky Point Arguello," Santa Ynez Valley News, September 17, 1954.

255. George W. B. Evans, Evans, Mexican Gold Trail: The Journal of a Forty-Niner (San Marino, Calif.: The Huntington Library, 1945), p. 197.

256. Ibid., p. 72.

257. Carey McWilliams, North from Mexico: The Spanish-Speaking People of the United States (New York: Monthly Review Press, 1961), p. 91.

258. Juan F. Dana, pp. 111-112.

259. Ibid., pp. 112-113.

260. Ibid., p. 112.

261. William H. Thomes, On Land and Sea, or California in the Years 1843, '44, and '45 (Boston: DeWolfe, Fiske & Company, 1884.), p. 303.

262. Frank Dana, "What Was Life Like on a San Luis Obispo Rancho? How did the Ranchero Make a Living?" <u>Nipomo News</u>, July 8, 1892.

263. Juan F. Dana, pp. 112-113.

264. Ibid., p. 113.

265. Ibid.

266. Frank Dana, "Frank Dana, Nipomo Rancho, 1840-1852," <u>Nipomo News</u>, July 22, 1892.

267. Ibid.

268. Juan F. Dana, p. 71.

269. Ibid., pp. 71-72.

270. William G. Dana and Josefa Carrillo de Dana, <u>Last Will and Testament</u>, December 26, 1853.

271. Benefield, p. 64.

272. Juan F. Dana, p. 95.

273. Ibid., p. 96.

274. Ibid., p. 97.

275. Juan Francisco Dana, "Ten Decades on a California Rancho: Random Memories of Stirring Events in the Golden State Under Three Flags," as told to John Edwin Hogg, <u>Touring Topics</u>, Vol. 23, No. 11, November 1831, p. 19.

276. Ibid., p. 16.

277. <u>The Larkin Papers: Personal, Business, and Official Correspondence of Thomas Oliver Larkin, Merchant and United States Consul in California</u>, ed. George P. Hammond, Vol. XV, October 1, 1845-May 31, 1846, pp. 306-307.

278. Ibid., Vol. VI, January 2, 1847-September 30, 1847, p. 2.

279. Thomas R. Tefft, "Episodes from the Short, Happy Life of Henry Tefft," <u>The Californians</u>, Vol. 10, No. 2, September/October 1992, p. 36.

280. Ibid.

281. Ibid., p. 38.

282. William Rich Hutton, Glances at California 1847-1853: Diaries and Letters of William Rich Hutton, (San Marino, Calif.: The Huntington Library, 1942), pp. 40-42.
283. Ibid., p. 43.
284. Ibid., p. 54.
285. Alonzo Patrick Dana, "The Beginning of Nipomo," Avila Beach Courier, undated.
286. Juan F. Dana, p. 41.
287. Alonzo Patrick Dana, "The Beginning of Nipomo."
288. Leo Carrillo, The California I Love: Leo Carrillo's Golden Cavalcade of California (Englewood Cliffs, N.J.: Prentice-Hall, 1961), pp. 107-109.
289. Thomas R. Tefft, p. 37.
290. Henry A. Tefft, letter to William G. Dana, December 12, 1849, in William G. Dana Papers, 1825-1858 (Bancroft Library).
291. Thomas R. Tefft, p. 39.
292. Henry W. Halleck, letter to William G. Dana, Halleck, Peachy, & Billings Records, 1852-1867, Bancroft Library.
293. Richard Beidleman, California's Frontier Naturalists (Berkeley and Los Angeles: University of California Press, 2006), p. 209.
294. The Larkin Papers: Personal, Business, and Official Correspondence of Thomas Oliver Larkin, Merchant and United States Consul in California, ed. George P. Hammond, Vol. IX, May 20, 1851-December 30, 1853, p. 204.
295. Yda Addis Storke, A Memorial and Biographical History of the Counties of Santa Barbara, San Luis Obispo and Ventura, California (Chicago: The Lewis Publishing Company, 1891), pp. 569-570.
296. William G. Dana, Correspondence and Papers, 1827-1849 (From the T.W. Norris Collection, Bancroft Library), letter of November 16, 1849.
297. Ibid.
298. William L. Beebee was appointed to replace him.

299. From Alonzo Patrick Dana, <u>California Pioneers: The Dana, Carrillo, Boronda, Deleissigues and Munoz Families in California</u>, 1ˢᵗ ed. (Arroyo Grande, California: 1966), p. 18.

300. Angel, p. 107.

301. Ibid., p. 105.

302. Juan F. Dana, p. 56.

303. Ibid., p. 60.

304. Ibid., pp. 61-63.

305. Ibid., p. 63.

306. William G. Dana, letter to Governor Mason, Nipomo, June 6, 1847, in <u>Unbound Documents</u>, Archives of California, Vol. 63, p. 168.

307. Ibid.

308. Luganda Cota, letter to William G. Dana, La Purisima, October 23, 1848, Dana Papers.

309. Ibid.

310. William G. Dana, letter to Joaquin Estrada, Nipomo, October 24, 1848, Dana Papers.

311. <u>Spanish and Mexican Land Grant Maps, 1855-1875</u>, California State Archives (from the United States Surveyor General for California).

312. William G. Dana and Josefa Carrillo de Dana, <u>Last Will and Testament</u>, December 26, 1853.

313. Samuel A. Pollard, letter to Abel Stearns, May 4, 1855, <u>Stearns (Abel) Papers, Collection I</u>, Huntington Library.

314. Alonzo P. Dana, p. 19.

315. Angel, p. 171.

316. Ibid.

317. Ibid.

318. Ibid.

319. Ibid.

320. William G. Dana, letter to John R. Cooper, San Buenaventura, July 13, 1828, Vallejo Documents, Vol. 29.

321. Juan F. Dana, pp. 55-56.
322. Walker, p. 31.
323. Juan F. Dana, p. 56.
324. Egan, p. 4.
325. Juan F. Dana, p. 70.
326. Ibid., p. 130.
327. Alonzo Patrick Dana, as told to Doris Olsen, "Nipomo: Dana Family Made History," San Luis Obispo County Telegram-Tribune, March 22, 1976.
328. Giffen, p. 56.
329. Ibid.
330. Ibid.
331. Ibid.
332. Juan F. Dana, p. 125.
333. Alfred Robinson, Life in California Before the Conquest, ed. Thomas C. Russell (San Francisco: The Private Press of Thomas C. Russell, 1925), p. 299.
334. Kevin Starr, Americans and the California Dream 1850-1915 (Santa Barbara and Salt Lake City: Peregrine Smith Inc., 1981), p. 42.
335. Richard Henry Dana, p. 72.
336. Ibid., pp. 72-73.

INDEX

Not all persons and places listed in the book are contained in the Index. And, for those individuals who were an integral part of William's life and are quoted or mentioned frequently, the page numbers given are for the first mention in each chapter, not for each time they are cited.

A

B

C

D

ABOUT THE AUTHOR

Joseph Dana, the great-great-grandson of William Goodwin Dana, has a longstanding interest in California history. He is descended from David Amos Dana, the 19th child of Captain and Mrs. Dana. Since 1999 he has been involved with the Dana Adobe Nipomo Amigos, a non-profit group working to create a Rancho Nipomo historic park with a restored Dana Adobe as the centerpiece. An elementary school principal in Orcutt, California, he has taken particular interest in introducing young people to the story of Captain Dana.

Dana holds a bachelor's degree in history from the University of California at Berkeley and a master's degree in educational management from the University of LaVerne. He and his wife, Angelina, have two children, Jacob and Sabrina. They reside in Orcutt.